GENERAL EDITORS

George and Louise Spindler

STANFORD UNIVERSITY

# PREDICTING THE PAST
*An Introduction to*
*Anthropological Archaeology*

**DAVID HURST THOMAS**
*The American Museum of Natural History*

# Predicting the Past
*An Introduction to*
*Anthropological Archaeology*

HOLT, RINEHART AND WINSTON, INC.
*New York    Chicago    San Francisco    Atlanta*
*Dallas    Montreal    Toronto    London    Sydney*

*To Marty, Red, and, of course, Trudy*

Library of Congress Cataloging in Publication Data

Thomas, David Hurst.
Predicting the past.

(Basic anthropology units)
Bibliography: p. 77
1. Man, Prehistoric.    2. Archaeology—Methodology.
I. Title.
GN739.T46        913'.031        73–7895
ISBN: 0—03—091154—0

# Foreword

THE BASIC ANTHROPOLOGY UNITS

Basic Anthropology Units are designed to introduce students to essential topics in the contemporary study of man. In combination they have greater depth and scope than any single textbook. They may also be assigned selectively to cover topics relevant to the particular profile of a given course, or they may be utilized separately as authoritative guides to significant aspects of anthropology.

Many of the Basic Anthropology Units serve as the point of intellectual departure from which to draw on the Case Studies in Cultural Anthropology and Case Studies in Education and Culture. This integration is designed to enable instructors to utilize these easily available materials for their instructional purposes. The combination introduces flexibility and innovation in teaching and avoids the constraints imposed by the encyclopedic textbook. To this end, selected Case Studies have been annotated in each unit. Questions and exercises have also been provided as suggestive leads for instructors and students toward productive engagements with ideas and data in other sources as well as the Case Studies.

This series was planned over a period of several years by a number of anthropologists, some of whom are authors of the separate Basic Units. The completed series will include units representing all the basic sectors of contemporary anthropology, including archaeology, biological anthropology, and linguistics, as well as the various subfields of social and cultural anthropology.

## THE AUTHOR

David Hurst Thomas is currently the Assistant Curator of North American Archaeology at the American Museum of Natural History in New York City. He received his formal education at the University of California (Davis campus), taking three degrees in anthropology (B.A., M.A., Ph.D.) from that institution. He has taught archaeology at the Universities of Nevada and California, and at the City College of New York; he is currently an Adjunct Assistant Professor at the City University of New York. He is also Associate Editor of *Human Ecology*, a new interdisciplinary journal. Professor Thomas has published several scientific papers discussing the rock art of the Great Basin, the analysis of food remains to reconstruct prehistoric diets, the application of numerical taxonomy and computer simulation techniques to archaeological theory, and the role of traditional scientific methods in archaeology. In addition, he is currently preparing a book on statistical methods in anthropology. Future research plans call for further archaeological excavation and survey in the central Great Basin, with an eye toward comparing prehistoric ecological niches of this region with those of other hunter-gatherer groups throughout the world.

## THIS UNIT

Archaeology, or *paleoethnology*, as David Hurst Thomas phrases it, is the study of cultural process and hence squarely within the framework of contemporary anthropology. But prehistoric processes cannot be studied directly, since the data of man's past are elusive and must be treated with various techniques before process can be the objective. This unit gives the reader an understanding of artifact classification, chronological control, and the reconstruction of past lifeways, because all of these techniques are necessary prior to studying process.

Paleoethnology bridges the gap between the past and the present and shows, indeed, how the present is relevant to the past. Without ever explicitly saying so, this unit shows how the best of the "old archaeology" can be wed with the "new archaeology" to form the total scientific study of man's cultural past. The very title of this unit, *Predicting the Past*, is diagnostic of this emphasis. This orientation is further promoted by the use of two Case Studies: one on the Washo by James Downs; the other on the Huron by Bruce Trigger. To help the student understand the relationship between the analytic presentation and what can be done with data from the past (or the present), the author provides a "Case Study Interaction" at the end of each chapter. The ingenious reader will see ways in which the basic purposes and procedures of these interactions can be applied to other materials, including his own culture and its products.

This Basic Unit should help the beginning student to avoid the misleading conclusion that archaeology is irrelevant to the present, or irrelevant to his own general education. Paleoethnology will be seen as an important pathway to a better understanding of man.

George and Louise Spindler
*General Editors*
STANFORD, CALIF.

# Preface

The following brief excursion into paleoethnology is grounded in the belief that well done is infinitely better than well said. Scientific archaeology, still in its virtual infancy, progresses haltingly and at this point has developed few steadfast principles. Anthropological archaeology currently lacks the firm body of theory which characterizes the more mature "hard sciences." As a result, this book proceeds largely by example, for I think that recent developments will chart the further direction of scientific archaeology. In considering these examples, we must operate at two rather discrete levels of discourse. Within the body of the text, several illustrations are considered in some detail in order to acquaint the beginning student with the archaeology of the real world. Paleoethnology alleges to study the cultural processes of mankind, for instance, but at this point archaeology has made relatively little substantive progress toward this end. The goal is a real one, however, and some recent projects are beginning to produce relevant results. I think it more important to consider a few such current attempts—such as the MacNeish and Binford investigations on the origins of agriculture and the Sanders-Price study of the evolution of Middle American civilization—than to expound in abstractions about potential aspirations. In fact, if the theories discussed here are not rejected completely, or at least substantively modified during the next decade, then I misread the current thrust of archaeology. It is questions more than answers which have given modern archaeology its new life as a viable social science. In this sense, *Predicting the Past* is an interim report, firmly dated 1974 and documenting the progress of current archaeology toward achieving its ultimate goals.

Yet this book also attempts to operate at a second level. It has been frequently emphasized that "archaeology is anthropology or it is nothing" (Willey and Phillips 1958:2). Not obvious to the uninitiated, however, is exactly how the dirt, bones, and stones of archaeology are in fact related to anthropology (too often considered the study of modern cultural exotica). To give the student a realistic assessment of archaeology *and* cultural anthropology, I opted to consider simultaneously material from *both* disciplines. This book is expressly designed to complement the Case Studies in Cultural Anthropology, the extensive monograph series published by Holt, Rinehart and Winston, Inc. Specifically, each chapter in *Predicting the Past* is concluded by a Case Study Interaction, a set of exercises which asks the student to integrate archaeological principles with solid ethnographic data. I have selected two companion volumes, to be used concurrently with this book:

*Two Worlds of the Washo* by James Downs
*The Huron: Farmers of the North* by Bruce G. Trigger

These two monographs, with their explicitly ecological perspective, provide ethnographic data suitable for archaeological integration. While the Interaction sections have been designed with these two Case Studies in mind, I welcome the innovative teacher to adapt his own preferences in Case Study material, consonant with his own background. Regardless of which ethnographic materials are selected, I cannot stress too strongly the importance of combining this volume, primarily archaeological in emphasis, with complementary studies from cultural anthropology.

I wish to thank many colleagues and friends for their help in preparing this book. Notable was J. Peter White of the University of Sydney, who generously allowed me access to his pioneering ethnoarchaeological study in New Guinea, upon which we had earlier collaborated. Dr. White is also to be credited with Figures 6, 7, and 8. The final draft benefited from critical comments by William Haviland, James Hester, and Frank Hole. This acknowledgment should not, however, be taken as indicating those scholars' endorsement of content or approach, for several of their suggestions were not followed. I also wish to thank my colleagues at the American Museum of Natural History for their help, especially Robert Carneiro, Gordon Ekholm, and Junius Bird. The following provided valuable leadership and experience to the Reese River Ecological Project in the central Great Basin (discussed in Chapter 5): Dan Andrews, Brian Hatoff, Bob Kautz, Randy Susman, and especially my good friend Len Williams. Thomas Layton of the Peabody Museum, Harvard University, provided me with my first taste of the dust of Great Basin archaeology and also permitted me access to his data from the Smoky Creek Cave (Chapter 4). Don Crabtree and the Idaho State University Museum provided the photograph of the Folsom replicas (Figure 5). I also thank David L. Clarke and the Methuen & Co., Ltd., of London for granting me permission to reproduce Figure 8, which appeared in *Models in Archaeology*, edited by Dr. Clarke. I thank Roberta Fischer for her assistance in preparing the manuscript. Finally, a hearty thanks to my wife and partner Trudy, whose patient hours of editing improved both syntax and logic, if not my disposition.

D. H. T.

# Contents

# 1
# Archaeology as Anthropology

Anthropology is the study of man embedded in his cultural matrix: *all* men in *all* cultures. Unlike most social sciences, anthropology does not attempt to narrow its scope by studying only selected societies within Western civilization. Neither is the subject matter limited to specific expressions of the human experience, such as economics, politics, child-rearing practices, and so forth. Unique among the social sciences, anthropology is *cross-cultural* in nature and *holistic* in approach. Since anthropology's goal is to generalize about all men in all places, anthropologists are likewise obliged to investigate men in *all times*. Although man evolved over 2 million years ago, he invented writing only within the last 5000 years. Surely no discipline touting itself as the universal science of mankind can ignore this bulk of man's story which remains unrecorded. The subfield of anthropology which studies these extinct cultural systems—paleoethnology—is the subject of this book.

Each major division of anthropology has evolved distinctive techniques with which to collect relevant data. Both the ethnographer and the linguist interact directly with living informants, conversing and questioning in order to garner cultural insights. The physical anthropologist likewise works with informants, but quite often the informant is mute (sometimes a skeleton) so that data are generally observed and measured rather than verbally elicited. Methodologically unique among the anthropological subfields, archaeology usually proceeds *without* informants; archaeologists can neither question a native speaker nor measure the proper bone or tissue of an informant's body. Archaeologists are restricted to viewing the material remains of extinct cultures through the selective lens of time. Archaeology is, as Heizer and Graham (1967) have suggested, the anthropology of the dead.

## HISTORICAL DEVELOPMENT OF ARCHAEOLOGY

Archaeology has advanced along a circuitous route in becoming the discipline we know today. Modern archaeology is an amalgam of diverse constituents, grounded primarily in British antiquarianism and early advances in the earth sciences.

The first gentlemen upon whom we can bestow the title of "archaeologist" were the looters and grave robbers of antiquity. In some cases, the grave had hardly been sealed when stealthy mercenaries purloined the sacred valuables from the tombs. Much of our knowledge of classical Greece, Rome, and Egypt has been induced from curios, originally looted, which miraculously ended up in some of the world's

1

large museums. The primary contribution, if it may be called that, of the early grave looters was their interest, albeit monetary, in the objects of the past. As ancient artifacts became more common, awareness of the past and its hidden secrets transcended pecuniary considerations.

Archaeology's greatest expansion came during the Renaissance when the leisured class of southern Europe, called *dilettantes*, indulged themselves with excavations of the tombs and mounds which dotted the European mainland. Artifacts of the past became the playthings of the rich. The focus of English antiquarianism of the 1700s, displaying a typical British restraint, confined itself by and large to mapping and recording the local Roman ruins and the pre-Roman barrows. Scientific organizations were formed, findings were published, and antiquities were preserved. Digging was minimal and the emphasis was squarely upon knowledge rather than acquisition of art objects. But the acquisition and study of ancient artifacts remained particularistic until Christian Thomsen, then Curator of the National Museum of Copenhagen, recognized the sequential evolution of the technology of mankind. The earliest artifacts were invariably made of stone, while the later Greek and Roman artifacts were often of bronze and other alloys. Only artifacts of relatively recent manufacture were made of iron. The definition of the ages of mankind (Stone, Bronze, and Iron) served as a framework within which to view the previously chaotic European archaeological finds. A second major breakthrough arose in historical geology when William Smith expounded the Principle of Superposition —that objects found lower in the earth will tend to be older. Such revolutionary insights ushered in a new era of systematic archaeology in the Old World.

While British archaeology was closely linked with the recognition of geological time, developments in the Americas took a rather divergent course. Early in the game, it became clear that American archaeology would never equal the European finds in sheer antiquity; man was indeed a relative newcomer to the New World. Even more significant than this was the implicit recognition of the continuity in the New World between the prehistoric past and the present. While the Europeans concentrated upon truly *ancient* stone artifacts with no apparent modern correlates, the American Indian was viewed as an analogy with which to interpret the artifacts and architecture of the past, as a living fossil. From the very beginning New World archaeology, unlike its Old World counterpart, was inextricably wed to anthropology through the study of living people; the vestiges of this distinction between European and American archaeology survive to the present.

In approaching the study of American archaeology, scholars were faced with several initial problems. Who were the first inhabitants of the New World? Where did they come from? And when? How do the spectacular ruins of Mexico and Peru relate to the nonagricultural groups of the far West? Can the American Indians be explained, as some suggested, as the twelfth lost tribe of Israel? In short, a comprehensive time-space sequence was necessary as the initial chapter in the unraveling of man's New World chronicle. Pottery sequences and tree-ring studies in the American Southwest provided the first of such solid chronological clues. In general, dating throughout the New World was tied into these few secure absolute dates from the Pueblos, a situation which remained unchanged until the advent of carbon-14 dating in the early 1950s. To the south in Mesoamerica, the deciphering of the Mayan calendar provided further chronological clues. In the pre-C[14] days, the Maya hieroglyphs were to the Mesoamerican archaeologists what tree-ring dating was to the Southwesterner. The recent proliferation of absolute chronometric techniques has revolutionized the establishing of local sequences and cleared the way for archaeology's progress to more strictly anthropological aims.

In a gross sense, then, the evolution of anthropological archaeology can be characterized by three sequential phases: from the archaeologist as a relic hunter, to the archaeologist as architect of cultural sequences, to the modern situation, with the archaeologist as a paleoethnologist.

## AIMS OF ARCHAEOLOGY

Although the overriding objectives of all anthropologists remain the same, the techniques which serve these aims are necessarily diverse: the cultural anthropologist relies upon his tape recorder, the linguist compiles grammars, while the physical anthropologist most frequently turns to metrical gadgets such as calipers, goniometers, and microscopes. But the most bizarre tool-kit in anthropology is surely that of the archaeologist. Aside from the ubiquitous shovel, trowel, and whisk broom, the archaeologist also calls upon dozens of ancillary aids in his study of culture: radiocarbon assays, x-ray diffraction, neutron activation, soil profiles, aerial photographs, and, recently, digital computers. Yet all these seemingly unrelated tools and techniques are tightly integrated into the overall fabric of modern archaeology, which can be characterized by three basic aims of archaeological research (after Binford 1968a): the construction of cultural chronologies, reconstruction of extinct lifeways, and the search for cultural processes. The primary aims of archaeology are both sequential and hierarchical, for no advanced level of investigation can be attempted until the preceding levels have been thoroughly considered.

In the anthropological perspective, archaeology's most salient asset is its *time depth*. The archaeologist can often analyze long and unbroken evolutionary sequences, developmental segments of culture which are unavailable to other anthropologists. While the ample time span may be archaeology's greatest boon, time is also the greatest obstacle. Before the paleoethnologist can turn to truly cultural and ecological aspects of the past, he must have a firm grasp upon time and archaeology's initial concern must always be the *construction of chronology*. If archaeology has a single inviolable rule, it is that one must know *when* before he can even consider *how*, *who*, *what*, or *why*. Controlling time generally involves two procedures: the classification of material remains, considered in Chapter 2, and the derivation of absolute and relative dates, discussed in Chapter 3.

After establishing a suitable foundation of chronological controls, the archaeologist moves to the second sequential aim, the *reconstruction of extinct lifeways*. While chronology is merely a stepping stone—something one *must* do—study of past cultural adaptations is directly relevant and compatible to modern anthropology. Reconstructing now-defunct modes of survival can be considered the ethnography of extinct societies, directly comparable with data collected from modern functioning societies. Lifeways are most frequently studied by intensive archaeological research in discrete regions; Chapter 5 presents a detailed example from the deserts of western North America to illustrate some of the objectives, tactics, outcomes, and potential pitfalls of one such regional project.

In addition to regional fieldwork, the archaeologist can study modern groups of primitive and/or non-Western peoples to gain insights into the mechanisms of past adaptation. The universities of modern industrial societies, while quite adequately preparing archaeologists for the intellectual rigors of scholarly research, are hard pressed to teach the basic human mechanisms necessary for coping with the environment; few city-educated people know how to work stone, fire pottery, stalk game, or boil water in a basket. This need to return to the basics has fostered the brand of archaeology known as "action archaeology." Unlike most other paleoethnologists, action archaeologists directly study viable, functioning societies in search of clues to understanding the past. At this point, the line between archaeology and general anthropology is a fuzzy one indeed. Since archaeology is deeply rooted in the study of material aspects of culture, it becomes vital to grasp the implications of primitive technology and, in so doing, archaeologists have learned to imitate methods of artifact manufacture lost for thousands of years. Chapter 6 discusses examples of action archaeology—a study of stone-tool manufacture in the New Guinea Highlands is one such project—to illustrate another analytical strategy of the paleoethnologist.

 Archaeology's third aim is also its most elusive: the search for *cultural processes*. No longer is archaeology content to merely observe, describe, and integrate; the modern archaeologist also wishes to *explain* the phenomena of the past. When dealing with either archaeological sequences or even extinct lifeways, the archaeologist confronts specifics—specific sequences or specific lifeways. Even the most articulate and well-reasoned discussion of a society's ecological adaptation remains a statement about a particular group, in a particular place, at a particular time—the phenomena are unique. To discuss the cultural ecology of the Great Basin (Chapter 5), for example, is to consider events bound in both time and space. But to discover the laws which govern adaptations of all men in similar habitats is to discover a universal. Archaeology's ultimate aim, the study of cultural processes, deals not with things unique, but rather with things recurrent. Anthropological archaeology's goals are thus timeless and spaceless, the final aim being to generalize about *all* men in *all* times. The systematic examination of alternative explanatory hypotheses is what makes the archaeologist a scientist rather than a historian.

# 2

# Classifying Material Culture

In pursuit of the anthropological goals of archaeology, the archaeologist is limited to observing those elements of man's natural and cultural milieu which preserve through time. Only rarely does the modern world have the opportunity to view the true splendor of a Pompeii; more often, all that remain are scattered bits of stone, bone, pottery, and dirt. Because they have relatively few obvious and tangible clues, pragmatic archaeologists have developed techniques which extract the last morsel of information from the existing artifacts and features. To fully appreciate the role of the paleoethnologist, we must first examine how he interacts with the only source of information he has—material culture.

Archaeologists excavate two kinds of specimens: artifacts and ecofacts. Artifacts are the material remains of cultural activities and early archaeology was almost entirely artifact oriented. Archaeological sites were often viewed as little more than "mines," areas from which to recover more and more artifacts. Within the last couple of decades however, the "person behind the artifact" has become as important as the artifact itself and American archaeology has shifted its emphasis from strictly establishing chronologies to also considering how people actually lived. This reorientation required a concomitant shift from an excavation design solely to recover artifacts to a field strategy concerned with recovering relevant ecological information as well. Bones, pollen grains, fish scales, seeds and leaves of plants are all of interest to the modern ecologically oriented archaeologist. For these data, Lewis Binford (1964) has coined the term ecofact. Modern archaeology can be said to be primarily involved with the recovery and subsequent analysis of artifacts, ecofacts, and their interrelationships.

When artifacts are removed from the ground, they are routinely assigned catalog numbers in the field. With their primary contexts thus recorded, the artifacts can be removed to the laboratory where the initial analytical step is to *identify* these objects wrested from the earth. Some forms of identification are relatively simple. Most of us would probably agree, for example, that the tiny triangular stone objects are probably "arrowheads," the flat porous items are sherds of "pottery," and those long, polished tubes must be "bone beads." Most excavators sort their specimens into such gross intuitive categories before leaving the field.

But in archaeology's analytical laboratory phase, the classifications must be more precise, relying upon detailed and well-defined criteria. The process of placing objects into existing groups is termed *identification,* a procedure which implies that suitable categories already exist. *Classification,* on the other hand, makes no such assumption. By classifying an object, one is forced to create his own primary groupings, to sort all of the unknowns into new divisions. There is a place for each of these analytical operations in archaeology. As a general rule, archaeologists *identify* ecofacts, since biological categories already exist and the archaeological specimens are merely fitted into the previously defined pigeonholes. Identifying ecofacts is thus a parasitic activity in which archaeologists temporarily don the biologist's lab coat in order to garner data necessary for environmental and cultural reconstruction. Such excursions into the world of natural science are discussed in more detail in Chapter 4, in the context of exploring extinct lifeways.

Artifacts, on the other hand, are most frequently *classified.* Only rarely can unknown artifacts be easily fitted into preexisting categories since such *a priori* groups require an established regional sequence. Classifying artifacts is generally group-forming in nature and requires a different operational procedure than identification. Artifact classification is thus a uniquely archaeological undertaking and as such requires more detailed attention.

There are, of course, several ways of classifying the same set of objects. To illustrate this, let us examine a familiar set of modern artifacts: a workshop of woodworking tools. The carpenter classifies his tools as hammers, saws, planes, files, drills, and spokeshaves, since he is primarily concerned with tool function. But when this carpenter insures his workshop, the insurance agent would employ another set of classifications; the same tools being sorted into new categories such as "flammable" and "nonflammable." The insurance agent may also assign each tool to yet another set of classes based upon estimated value: "under $10," "between $10 and $25," and so on. Should our carpenter decide to relocate his workshop, the furniture mover will group these same tools into new divisions such as "heavy" or "light," or perhaps "fragile" and "nonfragile." The point here—and the main point of archaeological classification in general—is that each classification must be formulated with a specific purpose in mind; archaeology has no general, all-purpose classification. As Irving Rouse (1970) has cogently expressed this problem, the archaeologist must continually ask himself "classification—for what?"

## TYPES OF TYPES

Archaeology's basic unit of classification is termed a "type." A rather specific concept, the artifact type is an abstract form, an ideal construct created by the archaeologist to facilitate analysis. Instead of considering the thousands of individual specimens recovered from an excavation, the paleoethnologist generally abstracts his data into a few dozen typological categories. Although the archaeologist excavates specimens, he analyzes types. There are many kinds of artifact types and the term "type" should never be applied without an appropriate modifier describing precisely *which* kind of type is being discussed.

## MORPHOLOGICAL TYPES

The most basic artifact type has been termed "morphological" by Julian Steward (1954). Also called "descriptive," these types are designed to reflect the *overall* appearance of an artifact. Morphological types attempt to define broad generalities (rather than focusing upon specific traits), simultaneously considering as many attributes as possible. Length, width, weight, material, color, and perhaps volume are just some of the attributes traditionally considered when defining morphological types.

Because of this generality, morphological types are of limited value as end products; their primary function is descriptive, to convey the appearance of a set of artifacts or features. In examining the range of material remains left by extinct social groups, many of the artifacts may be unfamiliar, often meaningless to the modern observer. The initial analytical step is a careful, accurate description of each artifact, grouped into morphological types. Consider, for example, one such description by Emil Haury, an eminent Southwestern archaeologist, in his site report on archaeological materials from Ventana Cave (Haury 1950:329):

> *Discs*—Of the twenty-four stone discs, twenty-two are centrally perforated. They were all made of schist, from 36 to 74 mm. in diameter and averaging 8 mm. in thickness. The customary way of producing them was by breaking and then smoothing the rough corners by abrasion. . . . Only one was well made. . . . Drill holes are bi-conical and not always centrally placed. Two were painted red. Next to nothing is known about these discs. . . .

Even though the function and cultural context of such stone discs remain uncertain, Haury illustrates and describes the specimens in enough detail so colleagues—both contemporary and future—can visualize the artifacts without actually having to view them personally. The basis of initial archaeological analysis is accurate description.

Not only are morphological types basically descriptive, they are also *abstract*. Types are not artifacts; a type is the composite description of many artifacts, each of which is quite similar. Every morphological type encompasses a certain range of variability. Several colors may have been applied, the quality of manufacture may vary, size often fluctuates, and so forth. Walter Taylor (1948:118) referred to this abstract quality as an *archetype*, emphasizing the rather elusive "ideal form" implicit in each morphological type.

In analyzing a prehistoric assemblage of tools, most archaeologists create morphological types as a first step, then incorporate these preliminary designations into *special-purpose types*, discussed later in this chapter. The initial sorting is usually rather informal, often consisting of merely tossing similar artifacts into piles upon the laboratory table. No attempt is made at this point to control contextual variables (stratigraphic association, cultural affiliation, etc.) for the primary concern is to create homogeneous groupings.

The procedural question which naturally arises is how many attributes to use. When separating pottery sherds from arrowheads, a single attribute will suffice: raw material. But when considering morphological criteria within these gross categories, several other attributes become potentially significant. For example, in a classification of morphological types of arrowheads, more specific attributes such as weight, sharpness, length, width, thickness, presence of side-notches, and patterns of flaking become critical. One must use as many attributes as necessary to achieve adequate separation of specimens. Morphological types have traditionally been based upon only a few, easily distinguishable characteristics. But recently, archaeologists have been demanding more of their types. Minute description has become the current norm and attribute lists are proliferating. In general, manual sorting becomes cumbersome and error-prone when more than about ten criteria are to be considered at once. Here the computer has begun to play a significant role. Using a set of empirical mathematical techniques known collectively as *numerical taxonomy*, archaeologists need only make the measurements and the machine will produce the morphological types. Such computer-assisted types are often superior to those created manually since hundreds of attributes can be considered, if necessary. Such morphological divisions are truly based upon *overall* similarity. Furthermore, when one uses so many attributes, it becomes less important precisely which attributes are chosen, thereby rendering artifact typology more stable and less subject to fluctuation between typologists. This technique, still in its infancy, can provide future archaeologists with as fine a set of morphological types as are required by the task (see Clarke 1968; Thomas 1971a, 1972a). Computer-derived morphological types are the same in principle as those formed by manually sorting artifacts upon the laboratory table. The basic difference is the degree of relevant detail. But regardless of how they are derived, morphological types form the basis for all further artifact classification.

## FUNCTIONAL TYPES

Upon hearing the word "hammer," most of us conjure up some sort of mental image. A verbal description of one such image could be:

a two-piece artifact, with a semirounded handle, generally made of hardwood. The handle, about one foot long, attached to a heavy metal casting, is flattened on one end and often scarred with battering marks.

The request to fetch such an implement would generally produce an object satisfying the above morphological description. But if that request came from a carpenter, our return might well be greeted by "Not the *claw* hammer. I want a *ball-peen* hammer!" All of our disparaging comments about "referential looseness" and "explicit definition" would do little to assuage the ruffled feelings because carpenters do not think in generalized morphological terms. They want a specific tool to fit the job at hand. The carpenter refers not to a morphological type but rather to a *functional type*. In general, morphological definitions are necessary to express *overall* differences—to separate hammers from saws—but their utility is hampered by the very generality which makes them necessary as the initial step in all classification.

In a small number of cases, the archaeologist is fortunate indeed because the *context of excavation* can give clues to artifact function. Chipped stone projectile points, for instance, can be used to tip spears, darts, javelin, or arrows, and archaeologists usually must guess function from the form of the artifact. But the lucky discovery of such an artifact lashed in its original binding dispels doubt as to function (at least in this one case). Another example of the importance of context is with so-called "bannerstones," which are finely polished slate artifacts, sometimes shaped like wings, other times looking more like small boats and often even appearing as birds, with long and highly polished beaks. The nineteenth century excavation of prehistoric curvilinear mounds of the eastern United States produced dozens of these objects, and bannerstones became widely known as *objets d'art*, but their function remained a puzzle until further excavation revealed a cache of bannerstones in a prehistoric grave. Each stone was lashed to the end of a spearthrower and the problem was solved—they were *atlatl* (spearthrower) weights, providing balance and thrust for proper propulsion of the javelin (Witthoft 1955).

It is unfortunate that such direct evidence for artifact function is a relatively rare event. More often, archaeologists are forced to divine function through analytical means, through the construction of *functional types*, more specialized and difficult to isolate than morphological types. While morphological types considered the overall, generalized appearance of a set of artifacts, a functional type focuses upon *specific* features. One example of this focus is the modern metalcutting implement, in which edge angle dictates the function. A penknife is a small tool with a rather delicate and sharp blade, which generally has an edge angle of about 10° and is well suited for either fine whittling or slicing. An axe blade is designed for heavy-duty chopping with a more obtuse cutting edge. The edge angle of a cold chisel is even duller. Each tool is suited for a specific purpose and these critical functional attributes are not interchangeable. Hardware stores would sell few pocket knives with blades shaped like tree wedges.

Edge angle measurements of prehistoric implements can likewise be good clues to their past functions. Apparently stone blades sharper than about 45° were often used for whittling or fine slicing of meat or hides. Edge angles ranging between 45° and 60° were best suited for skinning large animals, scraping skins prior to tanning, cutting wood, and shredding fibrous plants prior to basket weaving. Edges more obtuse than about 60° are generally attributed to heavy wood chopping or cutting extremely fibrous materials. Of course, edge angles vary between similar specimens, as do most metric attributes. It is also true that the degree of sharpness changes through use and stone tools are often resharpened, thus changing the angles. But in the long run, for a large series of tools, the measurements of the working edge, combined with the overall size—penknives are always lighter than axes—provides archaeology with quite serviceable functional types.

Microscopic examination has also proven useful for inferring prehistoric tool function. Specific tasks often produced diagnostic patterns of wear. Sometimes, such patterns are easily visible, such as the battering on the head of a steel hammer or the telltale scrapes and gouges on hacksaw blades. On stone tools, however, most of the use patterns are miniscule, requiring microscopic examination of the working edge. Stone knives, for example, were often employed to skin and then dismember the carcasses of large animals such as antelope, mountain sheep, and bison. While neither flesh nor bone is sufficiently hard to scratch and dull a stone knife, minute particles of grit, sand, and broken fragments of the tool itself clinging to the meat often score the working edge. Each cutting motion produces distinctive traces; hide scrapers usually receive parallel striations from the long, even strokes necessary for hide preparation, while scars on skinning knives tend to be more random. Patterns on drill tips are often circular and concentric. Such microscopic analysis is but another modern technique used by archaeologists to create functional types. Clearly, types formed in this fashion are more specific in intent than morphological types.

## TEMPORAL TYPES

A temporal type is a set of one or more morphological types with a fixed and known range in time. Temporal types allow both within-site and between-site dating, when more precise dating techniques such as the isotope methods of dendrochronology are unavailable.

Archaeological remains of known antiquity (artifacts, bones, features, etc.) were originally termed *fossiles directeurs* by the French. The bones of extinct Ice Age mammals, for example, were considered as index fossils, since any artifacts of man found in association with such extinct animals must have considerable (*i.e.*, Ice Age) antiquity. The earliest temporal types functioned to distinguish two gross categories of time: "very ancient" and "recent." Throughout the nineteenth century, more and more fossils were discovered until it eventually became apparent that the ancient river gravels of western Europe contained several forms of "antediluvian man." The oldest artifacts were large crude tools called *choppers*, little more than stream cobbles with a couple of strategic flakes removed to produce a sharp working edge. A bit later in time, a new artifact type appeared—finely chipped, triangular *hand axes*. There were several different kinds of hand axes (subtypes), each covering a discrete interval of time. Following the hand-axe age, a large variety of tools manufactured on flakes appeared; these fine artifacts coincided with Neanderthal remains and are called *Mousterian*. The next sequential phase was characterized by artifacts made upon narrow, specialized flakes called *blades*. The European sequence culminated in the manufacture of tiny *microblades*. Each of these distinctive artifact forms is a *temporal type*. Finding similar objects in a new, undated deposit allows the archaeologist to place the newly discovered stratum into proper chronological perspective. A century has elapsed since the first attempts by the French to impose temporal order upon the array of seemingly unrelated finds of exotic artifacts and extinct animals. Since that time archaeology has evolved rather standardized procedures for determining temporal types.

To establish a set of time markers, one first describes the individual artifacts in detail and groups them into morphological types. From this point forward, the archaeologist deals only with abstract categories—Taylor's archetypes—rather than with individual artifacts. The morphological types are then studied for significant temporal associations. If morphological type B is found only in strata dating between A.D. 500 and 1000, then morphological type B can be elevated to the status of a temporal type. When one finds several artifacts of temporal type B in future, undated contexts, the dates A.D. 500–1000 would be a plausible hypothesis for further investigation.

In practice, time markers are generally assigned names to facilitate their recognition. Arrowheads, for instance, can be termed "Eastgate Expanding-stem," "Gunther Barbed," or "Pinto Sloping-shoulders." In most cases, the first name indicates the site where the type was first recognized (the Eastgate Cave in central Nevada, Gunther Island in northwestern California, and the Pinto Basin in southern

California), while the second term is descriptive, denoting the most salient defining characteristic of the type. Similarly, pottery types are called by names such as "Troyville Stamped," "Withers Fabric-impressed," and "Churupa Punctated," all types which occurred at the Jaketown site in Mississippi.

The formation of temporal type is a somewhat *deductive* process (discussed in more detail in Chapter 7) in that trial groupings are delimited strictly upon the basis of form (morphological types) and then these abstract groups are tested for temporal significance against independent, stratigraphic data. Temporal types can thus be formed in a manner consistent with established "scientific" procedures.

All of us are surrounded by artifacts which can be viewed as temporal types: automobiles, soda bottles, newspapers, fashions in clothing, tools, and even wristwatches. Cars with running boards, for example, can be rather accurately dated as being manufactured before 1938 (± a couple of years). Dual headlights (two lights in each fender) appeared in about 1958, and massive rear fender "fins" were most popular during the 1957–1961 era. In the case of automobiles, the annual models are the morphological types, and temporal groupings can be formed by isolating descriptive categories into relevant time periods.

Archaeologists of the future, studying mid-twentieth century customs, will have hundreds of chronological clues beyond automobile parts. In well-preserved sites, the appearance of nylon and plastic will provide a post-1940 date, while other enterprising archaeologists will discover the potential of dating metal containers. The early tin-plated cans were supplemented in the 1960s by aluminum cans, so archaeologists (*contra* ecologists) will benefit from modern use of aluminum cans, since they preserve well through time. "Pop-tops" appeared in the late 1950s providing another chronological time marker. Zippers are a rather recent invention. Other fruitful areas of study will be the styles of book and magazine printing, advertising posters exhibiting a particular skirt length, single- versus double-breasted suits for men, and record jackets, to say nothing of the fads of the music itself.

Paleoethnologists have found that some kinds of artifacts make better temporal types than others. Waste chippage, hammerstones, and bone awls, for example, seem to change little through time so they are poor candidates for time markers. Pottery, on the other hand, reflects minute stylistic changes and provides the archaeologist with his most sensitive time markers. The pottery types of the American Southwest have been known for years and are well dated. Show an established Southwestern archaeologist a tiny potsherd and he can be expected to reply something like "Oh, Puerco Black-on-White, usually dates between A.D. 1050 and 1150, and the piece is probably from the Albuquerque area."

For the archaeologist, established time markers not only separate stylistic phases in time, but they also provide *fossiles directeurs*, which date associated natural and cultural remains. Further implications of dating by association are considered in Chapter 3.

## COGNITIVE TYPES

So far we have examined how artifacts are initially clustered into abstract groups, morphological types, and how these preliminary categories are subsequently fashioned into special-purpose types, either temporally or functionally significant.

We have yet to consider how such types relate to their cultural setting. That is, the types discussed thus far are pragmatic, isolated by archaeologists expressly to facilitate chronological control or to reconstruct economic activities. They are synthetic. But what can artifacts tell us about the minds of the people who actually made and used them?

According to the archaeologist James Deetz, in the mind of every artisan there exists an idea of the proper form that his handiwork should take, these psychological constructs being called *mental templates* (Deetz 1967:45) or *percepta* (Tugby 1958:24). The process of artifact manufacture translates this idea from the head of the maker to the raw substance of artifacts, whether it is volcanic glass, basketry material, or potter's clay. In a plastic medium such as pottery, finished artifacts are usually accurate reflections of the mental template, since errors can be readily corrected. But with more intractable materials such as stone and bone, the mistakes cannot be so easily corrected. If one accidently removes the wrong flake in manufacturing an arrowhead, he must either work around this mistake or discard the artifact to start anew. Some kinds of artifacts will hence reflect the mental templates better than others.

Templates are involved in both the manufacture and the use of artifacts and art styles. Our heads are full of mental templates. We all have ideas, cultural views of how things "ought to be." Oriental music sounds uncomfortably discordant to the average Western ear because the mental templates dictate alternative modes of harmony and rhythm. Cubism would have undoubtedly offended the Classic Greek eye. Even the generation gap reflects a clash between competing mental templates. In fact, much of our cultural world view is comprised of intersecting sets of personal mental templates.

To this point, the thrust of our discussion has proceeded from the artisan's mind through his hand to the finished artifact. But archaeological studies of ancient societies begin with the artifacts and can only work toward the mind. One must begin with a proper classification of the artifacts to discover what processes took place in the head of a prehistoric technician. When morphological types are combined to produce groupings which correspond to a mental template, the new categories are called *cognitive types*. In Deetz's terminology, a cognitive type is a *fossilized idea* and artifacts are a concrete physical manifestation of a mental template.

What is the relationship between these cognitive types and the other types we have discussed? Although several archaeologists argue that all temporal types are also cognitive types, I have separated cognitive types from all other categories since I personally do *not* think that patterning in time or function necessarily corresponds to a mental template. Consider the so-called "pop-top." This technological advance freed the average American from a messy can opener. When he wanted a beer, he merely pulled the ring. The early pull-tops were generally round, to facilitate an easy grip. But then authorities discovered that such pop-tops were being fed as "slugs" into telephones and parking meters instead of coins. The container industry was forced to change the design of pop-tops, making the rings oval-shaped or putting ridges around the sides, so the rings were no longer the same shape as coins. Pop-tops are thus a temporal type. The earlier type is round, the later type is either ridged or oval in outline. Archaeologists of the future should be able to use pop-tops as time markers to analyze the stratigraphy of twentieth century structures.

But do these temporal types correspond with a mental template? Are they cognitive types? Of course the decision-makers in the container industry had mental templates of oval versus round pop-tops, but most of the workers involved in the actual manufacture of the cans probably did not register the change as meaningful to them. But most important, since most of us (the users) are unaware of the minutia of pop-top lids—and many other subtle yet real differences which may have temporal significance—we cannot accept the premise that temporal types are always cognitively significant.

The cognitive type is thus a rather different concept than the other types we have considered. Mental templates and cognitive types are matters of the mind, products of the psychological make-up of an individual. If this person lived during a prehistoric period, then the mental template perished with the informant. Lewis Binford suggests that the study of extinct ideas be called "paleopsychology," an activity for which archaeologists are poorly equipped.

I do not mean to imply that archaeologists can never isolate cognitive types, since some of the time markers which archaeologists have isolated surely must have had cultural significance. But we can never *assume* that such differences were *always* correlated to mental templates. This correlation must be established in each case. We shall return to the complex subject of cognitive types and mental percepta in Chapter 6, when we shall examine some experiments conducted in the New Guinea Highlands among primitive stone workers. The New Guinea situation indicates that mental templates can be determined with a high degree of accuracy, but only through the guiding counsel of living informants. Extinct ideas may continue to fascinate archaeologists, but let us realize that such studies lie upon a different level of abstraction than temporal and functional typologies.

In summary, we have seen that archaeologists analyze abstract categories of artifacts called *types*. An artifact type is a grouping of similar specimens which have been isolated to answer a specific set of archaeological problems. No single set of artifact types can serve all functions simultaneously or with equal accuracy. A morphological type is designed for maximum generality, usually to facilitate initial description to reflect overall similarity between the individual specimens. Such generalized types are then usually regrouped and rearranged into special-purpose types, having functional and/or temporal significance. When confronted with a problem in chronology, the archaeologist needs temporal types which reflect minute stylistic changes, such as decorative motifs, pottery rim profiles, or arrowhead basal configurations. The study of lifeways requires a different typology based upon function, mirroring economic activities. Functional types rely less upon stylistically fluctuating attributes than upon the purpose for which the artifacts were originally manufactured: cutting, food storage, cooking, catching fish, sewing hides, carving wood, drilling holes. Functional types frequently exploit details on the "business end" of artifacts, especially edge angles and wear patterns. Functional pottery types are generally based upon shape and absolute size. A third specialized artifact type, the cognitive type, is considered when the archaeologist attempts to study idea systems and norms of the past. In ecological and cultural processual studies, cognitive types are only of peripheral usefulness. All types, however, have their place in modern archaeology and the point is that archaeologists must always be aware of which type fits the purpose at hand.

## CASE STUDIES INTERACTION

I.  In general, the only artifacts left in prehistoric campsites are imperishable objects of stone, bone, horn, and pottery. Historic sites also yield glass beads, metal objects, and occasionally even fragments of paper. In analyzing these items, paleo-anthropologists must be aware of two distinct, yet overlapping sets of material culture. The first assemblage, which George Cowgill (1970) terms the *physical consequences population*, includes all the items of material culture which are expected to result from particular human activities. But archaeologists can only hope to recover imperishable artifacts, so they are in fact limited to the *physical finds population*, those artifacts, ecofacts, and features impervious to deterioration.

   a.  Using data from Chapters 4 and 5 in *Two Worlds of the Washo*, construct the plausible artifact assemblages from a Washo winter village in the Carson Valley. Document your examples with page numbers.

EXAMPLE (only partially filled-in):

| Activity | Physical Consequences Population (Items present upon abandonment) | Physical Finds Population (Items present 500 years after abandonment) |
|---|---|---|
| Shelter | *galesdangl*:   winter house (p. 39) | House depression, possibly surrounded by stone circle |
| Hunting<br>•<br>•<br>•<br>• | Bow and arrow (p. 26)<br><br><br><br>Rabbit net (p. 27)<br>•<br>•<br>• | Stone arrowheads<br><br><br><br>No predictable remains<br>•<br>•<br>• |

   b.  Construct similar charts for (1) summer village on the banks of Lake Tahoe, (2) a temporary piñon gathering campsite, and (3) the site of a communal antelope drive.

II.  In *The Huron: Farmers of the North*, Bruce Trigger documents the dynamics of Huron warfare in almost grisly detail (especially Chapter 4). With this material as background, consider how archaeologists excavating a Huron village would reconstruct activities such as the war feast and the treatment of captives. Construct a chart which details the specific activities related to Huron warfare, describing the artifactual (and ecofactual) correlates in terms of both physical consequences and physical finds populations, as was done in Problem I.

# 3
# Establishing Chronological Controls

The Fourth Egyptian Dynasty lasted from 2680 to 2565 B.C. The Roman Colosseum was constructed between A.D. 70 and 82. In 1650, Archbishop James Ussher of Ireland proclaimed that God created the entire earth in 4004 B.C., at precisely 9 A.M. on October 23d. Each date represents the most familiar manner of chronological control, the *absolute date*. Such dates are expressed in a specific unit of scientific measurement: days, years, centuries, or millennia. But regardless of how the measurements are derived—Archbishop Ussher computed his estimate by projecting Biblical lifespans back into time—all absolute determinations attempt to pinpoint a discrete interval in time.

Archaeologists also measure time in a second, more imprecise manner through establishing *relative dates*. As the name implies, such temporal placement is not in terms of specific segments of scientific, absolute time but rather by a relativistic relationship: earlier, later, more recent, after Noah's flood, prehistoric, and so on. Often relative estimates are the only dates possible. We can be reasonably certain, for instance, that man's ancient ancestors discovered spoken language prior to the invention of the wheel; that is, language is *relatively* older than man's use of the wheel. Both forms of dating, absolute and relative, are means of controlling the dimension of time in the study of man's past.

In this brief survey, only a few dating techniques can be considered, and we are forced to ignore such important techniques as counting annual varves in geological deposits, dating through decoding the Maya calendar, and many of the important chemical methods such as the fluorine test, which was used in exposing the infamous Piltdown hoax.

## RADIOCARBON DATING

In 1949, the physical chemist Willard Libby announced to the world that he had  discovered a new physiochemical technique which would, when perfected, revolutionize absolute chronological controls in archaeology. For his discovery of the radiocarbon method, Libby later won the Nobel Prize in chemistry. The early radiocarbon dates were limited to measurements of materials younger than about 30,000 years, but subsequent technical refinements have extended the effective range of the "C-14" method back over 70,000 years.

The basic principles behind radiocarbon dating are relatively simple. Cosmic

15

radiation produces neutrons which enter the earth's atmosphere and react with nitrogen to produce the "heavy" carbon isotope C-14.

$$N^{14} + neutron = C^{14} + H$$

Carbon 14 is termed "heavy" because it contains 14 neutrons in the nucleus, rather than the more common load of 12 neutrons. The extra neutrons make the nucleus unstable and subject to gradual radioactive decay. Libby calculated that in every 5570 years, half the C-14 available in a sample will tend to decay; this time span is termed the "half-life" of carbon. Every time a neutron leaves a C-14 nucleus, a radioactive (beta) particle is emitted. The rate of C-14 decay can thus be measured by counting the number of beta emissions per gram of carbon.

$$C^{14} = B- + N^{14}+$$

With these fundamentals established, Libby could utilize radiocarbon decay as the basis for a chronometric tool. Plants and animals are known to ingest atmospheric carbon in the form of $CO^2$ (carbon dioxide) throughout their lives. When an organism dies, no further carbon is admitted into the body system, and that already present commences its radioactive decay. By measuring the beta emissions from the dead organism, one can compute the approximate length of time since that organism's death.

Due to the statistically uncertain nature of radiocarbon decay, C-14 dates are always followed by an error factor—the *standard deviation*. Since the chances of any particular molecule of carbon emitting its beta particle at a given time are almost infinitely small, the resulting errors can often reach significant proportions. A date of 1520 ± 25 years B.P.—read "1520 years before present, plus or minus 25 years"—means there is a two in three (67 percent) chance that the true date falls between 1495 and 1545 years ago. If one doubles the error factor to two standard deviations, there is a 95 percent chance that the actual date falls between 1470 and 1570 years ago. Standard deviation readings measure the consistency of the laboratory calibrations and must never be omitted from a C-14 date. If the standard deviation is too high, something is amiss with the date and perhaps it should be discarded.

The radiocarbon method is based upon several assumptions, one of the most significant being that both incoming solar radiation and the concentration of C-14 in the atmosphere have remained constant through antiquity. In an attempt to test these assumptions by considering samples of known age, Hans Suess of the University of California (San Diego) recently analyzed dozens of wood specimens from the bristlecone pine tree. Native to the western United States, some bristlecones live as long as 4600 years, making them the oldest living organisms in the world. Using dead tree stumps, a tree-ring sequence has been extended back nearly 8200 years by the techniques discussed later in this chapter. By dating bristlecone wood of known age, Suess compared the true ages based upon tree-ring count with those computed by the radiocarbon method. The results indicate that significant fluctuations *have* occurred in atmospheric C-14 concentrations; the assumption of C-14 stability is thus false and many previous radiocarbon determinations are in error. Dates younger than about 1500 B.C. seem to closely correspond with the tree-ring data, but radiocarbon dates prior to this time are in some cases 700 years too young. Because of Suess's work, such spurious dates can be recalibrated within the 8200 year range of the bristlecone sequence.

Most regional sequences are unaffected by Suess's correction factors. So long as *all* dating is by radiocarbon the various subareas will remain in identical relationship, the only change being to alter the absolute dating. American cultural sequences, for example, remain intact, although all appear slightly older in absolute time. The Old World, however, is not so fortunate because of a disparity in dating technique. In areas where writing was invented quite early, historic records provide the firm chronology, extending some 5000 years in length. Radiocarbon evidence for the Fertile Crescent and Egypt has been considered largely unnecessary as early chronologies relied upon the excellent historic sources. Western European chronologies, however, lacking historical records, were arranged strictly upon radiocarbon determinations. Over the years, Old World data have been almost universally interpreted as indicating that the early traits of civilization such as metallurgy and monumental funerary architecture were originally developed in the Near East, only later diffusing into the culturally retarded European area. The civilized Near Easterners were considered the inventors and the barbaric Europeans the recipients.

The Suess chronology changes much of that. In a recent discussion of this problem, Colin Renfrew (1971) suggests that the overall effect can be compared to a temporal "fault line." All of Europe, except the Aegean area, is now placed several centuries earlier, while the Greek and Near Eastern chronologies remain unchanged. Stonehenge, formerly considered the work of Greek craftsmen who travelled to the British Isles about 1500 B.C., is now dated *prior to* the rise of Greek civilization. According to Renfrew, Europe can no longer be viewed as the passive recipient of cultural advances from the Mediterranean heartland. The elaborate megalithic tomb complex in England, for example, now appears to date a full millennium prior to similar manifestations in the eastern Mediterranean area. Metallurgy may have even been developed independently in the Balkans. While diffusion of cultural traits is still considered important, the new dating often *reverses* the flow of such diffusion. The textbooks must be rewritten.

The Suess corrections are but a single example of possible sources of error in the radiocarbon method; other potential problems include recent nuclear tests, which change atmospheric levels of radioactive materials and burning of fossil fuels, especially coal and petroleum products, affecting the level of atmospheric C-14.

Despite careful scientific controls and assumptions, the radiocarbon laboratory can only date the sample submitted to them. The onus remains upon the archaeologist to provide relevant and uncontaminated samples. Extreme care must be taken to date only undisturbed areas of sites. There is also the problem of humic acid which, once formed in the soil, can contaminate all of the datable organics in that site. The *nature* of the materials submitted for dating is likewise important: wood charcoal seems the best, followed by well-preserved wood, paper, parchment, and so forth. Particular care must also be taken to prevent contamination of samples after extraction from the site. Samples are generally immediately placed in aluminum foil or adequately labeled sterile jars. Many archaeologists (myself included) will not permit smoking on or near an excavation, lest a future C-14 sample become contaminated. These procedures help guarantee accurate laboratory assay, but the responsibility is always upon the excavator to submit only significant samples and to interpret the results in light of other clues of dating. For a more complete consideration of the methods, assumptions, and applications of radiocarbon dating, see Hole and Heizer (1973, Chapter 12), Ralph (1971), and Willis (1969).

## POTASSIUM-ARGON DATING

A second type of absolute dating involves the decay of potassium (K-40) into argon gas (A-40). Rather than estimating the rate of radioactive emissions (as in C-14 dating), the K-A method determines the ratio of potassium to argon particles in rock. Since potassium decays through time, the more argon present, the older the rock. The initial datum in C-14 dating was the death of the absorbing organism, since C-14 acquisition ceases with death. Since the potassium-argon method is applied to rocks, however, the age estimate refers to the latest significant lithological change, usually in the form of vulcanism. (Faul 1971, Gentner and Lippolt 1969, and Miller 1969 discuss the K-A method in more detail.)

K-A dating involves assumptions not unlike those of radiocarbon analysis. There must have been no argon trapped at the time of formation, *i.e.*, all argon must be the direct result of potassium decay and all argon must be retained in the rock structure without absorption by the atmosphere. It is known that some rocks, such as mica, tend to leak argon, so care must be taken in deciding which rock types are subjected to potassium-argon dating.

The archaeological potential of potassium dating is also more limited than that of radiocarbon, since the K-A time range (as much as several billion years) is several times that of C-14. It is rare for archaeological deposits to exhibit such antiquity. Several important early man sites in Africa, however, have been successfully dated by K-A. At Olduvai Gorge, for example, the potassium-argon dates indicate that the *Zinjanthropus* fossils are roughly 1.75 million years old.

## DENDROCHRONOLOGY

Dendrochronology—tree-ring dating—was initially developed by A. E. Douglas, who was not an archaeologist at all, but rather an astronomer who was investigating the effect of sunspots on the earth's climate. Douglas knew that trees remain dormant during the winter and then burst into activity in the spring. In many species, especially the conifers, this cycle results in the addition of well-defined concentric growth rings, evident in the stumps of most trees. Since each ring represents a single year, it becomes a simple matter to determine the age of a newly felled tree by merely counting the rings. Douglas further reasoned that since the rings varied in size, cross sections should be informative about previous environmental conditions. The irregular tree-ring patterns over a long span of time could be pieced together from tree to tree, establishing a chronological sequence.

In this manner, Douglas began constructing a tree-ring chronology by beginning with living specimens, then overlapping this period with a somewhat older set of rings from another tree and so forth. But dead trees and snags provide a relatively small time depth, so the dendrochronology turned to the prehistoric record. Douglas initiated a project in which he combed the known archaeological sites of the American Southwest, looking for ancient beams and supports, taking samples where possible. Slowly, he was able to construct a prehistoric "floating chronology" which spanned several centuries but was not tied into the modern samples. With this sequence, Douglas could date various ruins relative to each other, but the hiatus between prehistoric and modern sequences defied efforts at absolute dating. So Douglas had to work with two separate sequences. The first could date with absolute precision almost all ruins younger than about the fourteenth century A.D., while the second relative sequence could only date sites in relation to one another. The older sequence was expressed through purely arbitrary numbers followed by the designation R.D. (Relative Date). But there remained "The Gap," that unknown span of time between the absolute and the ancient sequence.

At this point, the National Geographic Society, the American Museum of Natural History in New York, and the Carnegie Institution of Washington launched ambitious expeditions in an attempt to locate logs from the bothersome middle period. But the "Gap hunters," as they were called, experienced little initial success. Often the two sequences could be extended year by year, but the yawning Gap remained. The problem was that Pueblo peoples had lived in the large sites of Mesa Verde, Chaco Canyon, and elsewhere during the relative sequence, but then they abandoned these sites for parts unknown. The trail only became clear again in "post-Gap" sites occupied during the Spanish rule of the Southwest.

One clue seemed to be modern towns of the Hopi, where people had perhaps lived during Gap times. After suitable arrangements were made between the Gap hunter and the Hopi residents, borings were secured from the beams at Old Oraibi. The absolute sequence was extended back to A.D. 1260, but the Gap remained.

Finally in 1929, the archaeologists turned to the modern villages in eastern-central Arizona. A rather unappetizing place to dig, the archaeologists excavated the Showlow site, located amidst the disarray of contemporary pigpens and corrals. But finally a small charred log was found, preserved in paraffin and labelled HH39. Upon checking, Douglas discovered that HH39 neatly "bridged the Gap." The last year of the relative sequence was established at A.D. 1284. With the sequences united and the Gap disposed of forever, the spectacular ruins of the Southwest could be dated with impunity: Mesa Verde had been occupied from A.D. 1073 to 1262, Pueblo Bonito in Chaco Canyon from A.D. 919–1130, the Aztec Ruin from A.D. 1110–1121. Since that time, the dendrochronological sequence of the Southwest has been extended to a range of almost 2000 years, and local sequences have been established for other areas, including Alaska and the Great Plains.[1]

It can be seen that tree-ring dating provides absolute dates for archaeological

[1] An amusing and rather ironic sidelight to the Showlow story is that when HH39 was added to the picture, the former absolute and relative sequences were found to *overlap 49 years*. Apparently a long period of drought during the thirteenth century had formed rings so minute that they had been previously overlooked. That is to say, there had not been a Gap at all! The data had been there since the earlier expedition to the Hopi town of Oraibi, but it took a clear-cut specimen like HH39 to clarify the sequence. For a lyrical and charming personal account of the Gap hunters, I highly recommend the book by Ann Axtell Morris (1933), wife of archaeologist Earl Morris and an early Southwest explorer in her own right.

sites, subject to the important limitation common to all such dating methods, for there must always be a clear association between the datable specimen and the cultural materials. One must assume that the wood was timbered at the time of occupation, since the use of dead trees or beams from abandoned structures can provide erroneously ancient dates.

Matching unknown specimens to the regional master key has been a slow laborious process requiring an expert with years of experience. Gradually more automated means such as correlation graphs have been devised, and recently computer programs have been written (based upon the statistical theory of errors) so that undated sequences can be statistically fitted into the master sequence.

In addition to providing calendar dates for sites, dendrochronology likewise has potential for providing climatic data. If tree-ring width is controlled by environmental factors such as temperature and soil moisture, then one should be able to reconstruct past environmental conditions by examining the band widths. Tree metabolism is a most complex process, and progress in ecological reconstruction has not provided as many answers as could be desired. Perhaps the more sophisticated means of automated tree-ring analysis will provide more satisfying results in this area. (I suggest Michael 1971 as a reference for further reading on dendrochronology.)

## DATING BY ASSOCIATION

Often the archaeologist cannot use isotope or tree-ring dating, either because proper material is lacking or because funds are unavailable—C-14 and K-A dating are quite expensive. One is then forced to rely upon relative chronological means. Dating by association is probably the most frequently applied dating technique, albeit less reliable than the various isotope techniques. One method of association dating is through the use of *time markers*, artifacts of known age used to date unknown strata within a site. Time markers, discussed earlier in Chapter 2, are generally artifact types or bones which have been satisfactorily dated in other contexts. It seems clear, for example, that the New World mammoth became extinct in North America about 10,000 years ago (Martin 1967:97). Finding a mammoth in a new excavation leads the archaeologist to suspect that his site may be older than about 8000 B.C. Similarly, the archaeologist who digs up several knives chipped from bottle glass will be inclined to assign a historic date to that portion of his site. Both the mammoth bones and glass scrapers thus function as time markers, or index fossils.

Dating by association is particularly subject to errors in both excavation and interpretation. Discovering a single time marker in a site must be viewed with a healthy skepticism until the initial find is confirmed by additional specimens. The most obvious source of error is due to sloppy excavation techniques, in which stratigraphic levels have been accidentally mixed. Sometimes the mixture occurs prior to excavation; rodents such as pack rats, for instance, are notorious for moving artifacts throughout the strata of a buried site. A single time marker can *never* be trusted.

*Read before Test*

## SERIATION

Another form of association dating is the *seriation* technique. A relative chronological method, seriation only places stylistic periods as *relatively* earlier or *relatively* later than another. Seriation does not allow the archaeologist to estimate *how much* time separates two such periods. In other words, the absolute dating techniques such as C-14 and K-A are quantitative while seriation remains only qualitative.

The implicit assumption in seriation is that prehistoric peoples, like their modern descendents, are fickle in matters of style. New ideas are commonly rather slow to catch on with only a few pioneering individuals participating in the fad. But fads have a way of gaining popularity within a group, and becoming superimposed upon earlier vogues. Popularity is a fleeting thing, however, and by their very nature styles fall into disuse. If one were to graph the relative popularity of a series of fads, it would become evident that they often form a characteristic curve (see Figure 1). Styles are gradually introduced, flourish, and then slowly disappear, producing a curve which is pointed on both ends and largest in the middle. This popularity curve, which archaeologist James Ford characterized as "battleship-shaped," seems to have cross-cultural universality and forms the basic assumption of seriation. By arranging a series of temporal types into such lozenge-shaped curves, one can establish a *relative chronological sequence.*

Seriation has proved most useful in establishing chronological ordering in a series of discrete archaeological contexts (sites), representing several overlapping temporal periods. Such a situation is most frequently encountered with preliminary data from surface surveys. The seriation procedure can be briefly outlined as follows:

1. Classify the artifacts into temporal categories.
2. Compute the relative popularity of each category (percentage frequency) within each site assemblage.
3. Order the sites so that the percentages for each type tend to grade smoothly into each other, forming the types into battleship-shaped curves.

The inference is that this linear ordering is a chronological sequence. It only remains for the archaeologist to determine which end of the sequence is "early" and which is "late," a final step based upon data external to the seriation.

Let us now consider a hypothetical example which illustrates such procedures. An archaeologist interested in investigating cultural changes which occurred during the period of White-Indian contact has discovered five historic Indian sites. If he can first order these sites in time, he can then determine the changes in group size, subsistence patterns, and material culture in general. A detailed surface survey was conducted on each site, and the surface artifacts adequately sampled. As is often the case in archaeology, only enough money is available for excavation of three of the five sites. In order to get an adequate picture of acculturative process, it is desirable to excavate sites from different time periods, so it is first necessary to order the five sites on a temporal continuum.

The most common artifact in historical sites is generally glass from broken bottles, windows, and other household items. In order to seriate the five sites on the basis of the glass recovered, it is first necessary to define a set of *modes*, the ways in which glass fragments differ from each other.

1. *Color.* Although antique bottle collectors have stripped all of the complete bottles from the sites, the surface is littered with glass sherds. These fragments seem to be of basically two colors. One kind is the crystal-clear glass common to most modern bottles and the other kind of fragment has a distinctive purple cast. Although this purple glass was originally clear at the time of manufacture, exposure to sunlight has reacted with the manganese oxide in the glass to create the purple color. Since manganese was added to the molten glass mixtures only prior to World War I, glass color can be considered a temporarily significant mode.

2. *Pontil marks.* Many of the glass fragments are the bottoms of old bottles and some have a rather distinctive scar known as a *pontil mark.* A pontil is a long iron rod which was formerly used to hold bottles during the finishing process. The bottle was empontilled after removal from the blowpipe so that the bottlemaker could add the additional glass necessary to finish the neck. It was necessary to give the iron rod a sharp tap in order to detach the finished bottle from the iron pontil, and as a result, empontilled bottles all have a rather jagged scar on the outside of the bottom plate. Pontils were gradually replaced by devices called *snap cases*, which gripped unfinished bottles about the body rather than upon the bottom. Thus bottles made with a snap case have no pontil mark. Historic records show that snap cases were introduced in the United States during the late 1840s and had almost completely super-ceded the pontil by 1870 (Jones 1971). As a result, bottle bottoms lacking pontil marks found in archaeological sites can be considered post-1870, while the bottoms bearing pontil marks are generally older than about 1850–1870.

3. *Bottle seams.* During the nineteenth century, bottles were generally begun on a blowpipe and then formed in a two- or three-piece mold. At the joints, small ridges (*mold marks*) were left in the process of manufacture. It was then necessary to add the lip of the neck in a separate process. After about 1850, a *lipping tool* was used; this consisted of a plug placed into the unfinished neck and two "forming arms" which clamped about the outside of the neck. As the lipping tool rotated, it simultaneously smoothed the lip, removed the mold lines from the neck, and left the glass with a swirled appearance. Hence in bottles made after about 1850 the mold marks were obliterated on the bottle neck. In 1903, a completely automated bottle machine was patented, which produced bottles in a single mold. By this new process, the mold marks ran up the neck and onto the lip. The invention caught on quickly and by 1920 the changeover was essentially complete, save for a few bottles produced by hand as novelties. Bottle necks found with mold marks runnings onto the lip can thus be dated to the twentieth century (Lorrain 1968).

Through careful analysis of the glass refuse, the archaeologist can derive a chronology by *seriating* the collection, assuming that each historical site was adequately sampled. Had the archaeologist just poked around haphazardly, picking up only the large or brightly colored glass fragments, significant bias could have easily resulted. Table 1 presents the quantitative counts of glass fragments from the hypothetical sites.

The trickiest aspect of any seriation problem is to convert the table of percentages into the proper relative order. This means the sites (rows) must be rearranged so that the percentages grade into each other. When one has only a few sites and types, as in this simplified example, the table can be cut into strips, so that each row

TABLE 1.    MODES OF BOTTLE GLASS FROM FIVE HISTORIC ARCHAEOLOGICAL SITES

| Sites | Total Fragments | Modes | | | | | | | |
| | | Purple Glass | | Pontil Mark | | Seam on Lip | | No Seam on Lip | |
| | | No. | % | No. | % | No. | % | No. | % |
|---|---|---|---|---|---|---|---|---|---|
| Pete's Summit | 903 | 452 | 50 | 181 | 20 | 90 | 10 | 271 | 30 |
| Pony Canyon | 462 | 139 | 30 | 46 | 10 | 139 | 30 | 92 | 20 |
| Cold Springs | 1096 | 658 | 60 | 548 | 50 | — | 0 | 438 | 40 |
| Stony End | 763 | — | 0 | — | 0 | 458 | 60 | — | 0 |
| Cripple Creek | 876 | 88 | 10 | — | 0 | 350 | 40 | 88 | 10 |

is on a separate piece. These strips can then be rearranged in different orders until one finds the smoothest ordering. When several sites and/or types are involved, however, this method becomes too cumbersome and several computation techniques have been implemented. Computer programs exist which can simultaneously deal with hundreds of sites and artifact types.

Figure 1 is a seriation diagram, which has placed the sites into their proper chronological order. The battleship-shaped monoliths are typical for seriation diagrams, indicating when artifacts come into use, become more popular, and then trail off in frequency as they are replaced with new styles. The relative order of sites is therefore: Stony End, Cripple Creek, Pony Canyon, Pete's Summit, and Cold Springs. But nothing in the seriation method tells us which end of the sequence is earlier, Stony End or Cold Springs. The archaeologist must resort to ancillary data to determine the directionality. In this case, we know that Cold Springs must be the most ancient site, in view of the high proportions of the older artifact modes, especially purple glass (60 percent), and bottle necks lacking mold marks (40 percent). The graph grades from the earliest (bottom of the diagram) to the latest site, Stony End.

Using this relatively simple method of seriation, the archaeologist can obtain a serviceable sequence of these historic sites, and he can presumably make an intelligent decision regarding which sites to excavate. If he wishes to pick the earliest, the latest, and an intermediate site, he will decide upon the Cold Springs, Stony End, and Pony Canyon sites. It is a truism that modern archaeology is coming to rely upon logical, data-oriented decisions and less upon intuitive guesses.

## CASE STUDY INTERACTION

I.    Contact with White-Anglo culture was disruptive for the Washo Indians. Since the earliest historic encounters, the Washo have been a people in flux, in a varying yet continual state of cultural change. Social changes of this sort are of interest to anthropology because the dynamics of culture is a primary vehicle for understanding cultural processes. Fortunately, the Washo case has been well documented by historic sources such as settlers' journals, contemporary newpaper accounts, and also by early anthropological fieldwork. But in the millions of years of man's evolution, most instances of cultural change lack such documentation. If the anthropologist is to make use of any prehistoric examples of significant cultural change, he must first

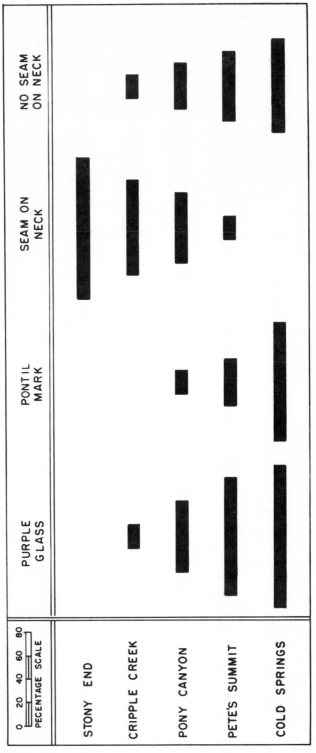

Figure 1. Seriation diagram for hypothetical historic sites.

be able to control the temporal variable; it makes little sense to study episodes of change if one cannot discern "earlier" from "later."

Forgetting for the moment that we have documentation for the Washo, let us examine evidence from historic Washo archaeological sites. Since the time span is too short for C-14 or K-A dating, and since no dendrochronological sequence exists for the central Sierra Nevada region, dating must rely upon artifacts which systematically vary through time—*temporal types*. Let us assume that Washo cultural change can be divided into three time periods:

1. From 1826 (Jedediah Smith's arrival) to about 1890.
2. From 1890 to the 1920s.
3. From the 1920s to the present era.

Restricting your attention to Chapters 8 and 9 in *Two Worlds of the Washo*, find at least one dozen temporal types for *each* of the three chronological periods. Arrange your answer in tabular form, indicating which artifacts could be expected to preserve through time.

EXAMPLE (only partially completed):

| Time Period | Physical Consequences Population | Physical Finds Population |
|---|---|---|
| *1.* 1826–1890 | 1. Rifles (p. 82) | rusted metal gun fittings |
| | 2. Cloth dresses (p. 88) | manufactured buttons |
| | • | |
| | • | |
| | • | |
| | 12. | |
| *2.* 1890–1920s | 1. Shotguns (p. 83) | rusted metal shotgun fittings |
| • | • | • |
| • | • | • |
| • | • | • |

II. In *The Huron: Farmers of the North*, Trigger (pp. 21–25) discusses the evolution of Northeastern Indian settlement patterns over the last 1000 years.

    a. Using this discussion as your data, divide Huron prehistory into at least four temporal periods and outline the important events in each period. Include probable artifacts, ecofacts, and settlement pattern shifts.

    b. This Huron sequence has been frequently dated by archaeological dating methods. Considering the chronological controls discussed in this chapter, which techniques would you imagine were of the most help in dating the prehistoric Huron sites? Discuss the advantages and disadvantages of each method used in studying the Huron's ancestors.

# 4

# Reconstructing Past Lifeways:
## *Techniques*

To an archaeologist, a *lifeway* includes all the diverse ways in which a people relate to their total natural and cultural environment. This includes the acquisition and preparation of food, use of land, how people distribute themselves across the landscape (demography), the manufacture and use of tools, daily dress, trade with neighboring and distant groups, competition for food resources, relationships between man and other creatures. In short, to describe a lifeway, be it prehistoric or contemporary, is to consider the place of a social group in its ecosystem.

The archaeologist has evolved a highly specialized battery of data-collecting techniques to unravel prehistoric lifeways. In any scientific pursuit, some questions are more likely to be answered than others and experience has taught the archaeologist precisely which questions to ask of the archaeological record, and what data must be gathered to provide the answer. Bald data cannot and will not speak for themselves. This chapter considers only a fraction of the possible techniques which can be applied to the remains of the past.

## ANIMAL REMAINS

Probably the most common noncultural debris in archaeological sites is faunal materials, such as shells, bones, fish scales, and coprolites (fossilized feces). Current standards of archaeological research pay strict attention to these ecological clues. A few decades ago, it was rare indeed to find an excavator saving any nonhuman remains from his sites. The spectacular finds, such as the bones of a mammoth or an extinct form of bison were usually preserved, but the majority of the faunal material was shovelled out to facilitate more rapid recovery of the "really important" cultural materials (the artifacts). Recent interest in ecological aspects has spurred fieldworkers to refine their recovery techniques. Where archaeologists formerly saved only unusual animal remains, many investigators now insist upon saving *every* scrap of faunal materials.

The first step in analyzing faunal samples is to separate the human food items, those resulting from prehistoric economic activities, from elements introduced by noncultural agents such as pack rats, coyotes, and owls. Bone is often the most plentiful and informative faunal remnant in an archaeological site, so it is critical to distinguish food remains from extraneous elements. Of some aid in making this distinction is the evidence of burnt bones, butchering marks from stone tools, and breakage patterns, since bones were often systematically fragmented to extract the nutritious and tasty marrow.

Once the food bones are satisfactorily segregated, several lines of analysis are open. One technique calls for the determination of the "minimum number of individuals" involved. By counting the bones and determining the most frequent body element represented, it is possible to calculate the minimum number of animals required to provide the total number of bones excavated. Carl Gustafson of Washington State University applied this method to bones recovered from the spectacular Ozette Village site, located on the Northern Pacific coast. Over 80,000 mammal bones were recovered, about 80 percent of which were *Callorhinus ursinus*, the northern fur seal (Gustafson 1968). After a suitable sample was taken, Gustafson determined the approximate number of individuals involved by counting the frequency of each skeletal element present. He found that the canine teeth seemed to be the most abundant body part present at Ozette. It was clear that after the left and right canines were sorted into matching pairs over 1000 individual fur seals had been killed at Ozette. The age and sex structure of the fur seal population was reconstructed and a prehistoric migratory pattern suggested. Through his careful analysis, Gustafson shed a bright light on the hunting techniques and traditions of the prehistoric Northwest Coast Indians of Washington.

Careful faunal analysis can also offer the perceptive archaeologist a glimpse at prehistoric butchering patterns. At the Glenrock Buffalo Jump site in Wyoming, archaeologist George Frison (1970) excavated a kill station which contained thousands of bison bones, many of them broken and scored in the butchering process. After removing the hide, hunters hacked through the base of the large muscles so they could more easily cart off the large meaty portions. Leg bones were removed, presumably to be crushed into a heavy smelly bone grease. The internal organs were retrieved from the body cavity; skulls were then opened, the tasty brain removed perhaps to be devoured on the spot. Frison suggests that since few tail vertebrae were recovered, the tail may have remained attached to the valuable hide or perhaps the tails were cut off by the victorious hunters and kept as odoriferous trophies. The entire butchering process can thus be reconstructed by minute examination of the bones recovered from the site.

Animal remains in archaeological sites can also yield clues about prehistoric food intake. One such analysis of bones was made to determine the approximate protein contributions of several species of mammals to the diet of the prehistoric denizens of the Smoky Creek Cave in the high deserts of northern Nevada (Thomas 1969a). It is clear that a mouse bone represents somewhat less meat consumed than does an antelope bone, and to correct for this size bias, total counts of fragments must be multiplied by the meat available for each species. Deer, for example, provide about 100 pounds of usable meat per animal, while jackrabbits contribute only about 3 pounds for each individual. This means that one must kill over 30 rabbits to obtain as much meat as that available from a single deer carcass. These numbers have been combined into a chart indicating the relative importance of food animals hunted around the Smoky Creek Cave. Figure 2 indicates that mountain sheep (*Ovis*) declined in overall dietary importance at Smoky Creek, while cottontail rabbit (*Sylvilagus*) increased markedly in significance. The bottom of the site (150

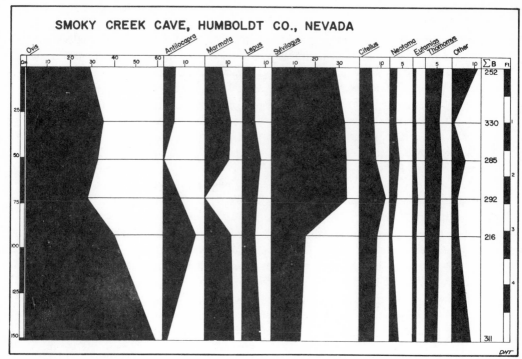

*Figure 2. Protein intake proportions from Smoky Creek Cave in western Nevada (reproduced from Thomas 1969a).*

cm.) dates about 1000 B.C. and the site was totally abandoned about A.D. 600, so apparently the decrease in the importance of mountain sheep occurred about A.D. 1 in this site. Whether this change is due primarily to environmental shifts with their concomitant shifts in biotic communities or to a different focus in hunting patterns remains undetermined.

Bones and shell can also provide the archaeologist with an estimate of *seasonality*, the time of the year when a site was occupied. In a classic example of faunal analysis, Hildegarde Howard (1929) demonstrated the potential of such noncultural remains for reconstructing lifeways by identifying the avifauna (birds) from the Emeryville Shellmound on the San Francisco Bay. Howard identified several of the bones as cormorants, birds which nest on offshore islands in the early summer. These nestlings move on shore after about a month and it is here that they were killed by prehistoric hunters. Howard reasoned that since the bones found in the mound were of relatively immature birds, the prehistoric hunts must have taken place between the middle of June and the end of July. Cormorants were found throughout the midden, so Howard concluded that the site was probably occupied most frequently during the summer. This early example of paleoecological reconstruction has been emulated by many archaeologists in the decades since Howard's pioneering work.

Margaret Weide (1969) used a somewhat different technique to attain similar results at the Edwards Street shell midden on the southern California coast. The most common molluscan species present was the Pismo Clam (*Tivela stultorium*). Weide noticed while excavating the site that the shells were remarkably uniform in size and shape. After further investigation, she discovered that such uniformity is because the clams had been harvested at the same time each year. Like trees, clams add growth rings each year, so a careful examination of such shells can disclose when growth ceased (when the harvest took place). Weide determined that the bulk of shell collecting at the Edwards Street site must have occurred during January, although the total gathering season probably extended from late winter through early spring. It seems ironic that archaeologists are often able to determine seasonality within an error of a few weeks, and yet sometimes cannot determine the absolute age of the site within several hundred years. It is as though we could look at a clock and see that it is exactly 35 minutes after the hour, but we are unable to tell whether this hour is 2, 3, or 4 o'clock.


## PLANT REMAINS

The analysis of ancient plant pollen and spores, known as *palynology*, has recently become one of the archaeologist's prime methods for examining prehistoric ecological adaptations. Most plants shed their pollen into the atmosphere, where it is rapidly dispersed by wind action. Pollen grains are thus present in most of the earth's atmosphere including, of course, archaeological sites. Small wonder, since a single pine branch produces as many as 350 million individual pollen grains.

While the interpretation of pollen concentrations is quite difficult, the initial steps in extracting and identifying pollen are rather simple. Pollen samples are generally taken from the sidewall of test pits or trenches, special care being taken to prevent contamination of the sample with foreign pollen. A suitable sample generally consists of a fist-sized dirt clod called a *ped*. Samples are usually taken at 5 or 10 centimeter intervals to provide a continuous record of the pollen rain throughout the period of deposition at the site. Careful stratigraphic drawings are made to facilitate correlation between the pollen record and the archaeological remains. The pollen grains are isolated in the laboratory through use of acid baths and centrifuging. Microscope slides containing the fossil pollen grains are then scanned and analyzed. The standard procedure is to identify and enumerate the first 200 pollen grains encountered on each slide. These figures are converted to percentages and integrated into a *pollen spectrum*, indicating the proportional shift between stratigraphic levels within the site. The pollen profiles are then correlated with the known absolute and relative dates for each stratum.

The pollen diagram can be interpreted for various purposes, the most common of which is the reconstruction of past environments. The archaeological samples are statistically compared with the pollen rain from known extant plant communities. The ratio of tree to nontree pollen, for example, generally indicates the degree of forestation. Pollen percentages which fluctuate through time indicate shifts in prehistoric habitats. The postglacial climatic sequence in Europe, well known from hundreds of pollen samples, contains notable fluctuations in the forest cover, as indicated by the frequencies of hazel, oak, birch, and grass pollen.

Once several pollen diagrams from an area have been analyzed and integrated, a *regional sequence* can be constructed. At this point, pollen analysis can be considered a *relative dating technique.* An undated site can be placed in proper sequence by simply matching the unknown pollen frequencies with the dated regional frequencies, just as in dendrochronology. In eastern Arizona, pollen analysis has even assisted in the reconstruction of the sequence of pueblo room construction (Hill and Hevly 1968). The regional pollen profiles indicate that during the occupation of the Broken K pueblo from A.D. 1100 to 1300, the relative frequency of tree pollen was decreasing. Through careful excavation, the floors of about fifty rooms were located and pollen samples taken. Samples from room floors are assumed to represent the pollen rain during site occupation. Each room was placed in proper temporal sequence by measuring the relative frequency of tree pollen, since earlier rooms had higher arboreal pollen counts than did the later rooms. The sequence of room construction compiled in this fashion corresponded precisely with the sequence based upon architectural superposition and soil stratigraphy.

Analysis of Broken K pollen also provided another unique application of palynology. Hill and Hevly were able to isolate room functions through the analysis of the fossil pollen spectrum. During the excavation of the site, it became clear that several different sorts of rooms were represented. Many of the rooms contained fire hearths and stone slabs for grinding corn; these were interpreted as habitation rooms, where daily activities generally occurred. A second type of room, considered a storage facility, was not only smaller than the habitation rooms but also lacking in the artifacts and features involved in food processing. A third type of room, markedly different from the others, was round in plan view and completely sunken below the ground surface. Both context and artifact yield convinced the excavators that these rare rooms must have been ceremonial, analogous to the modern pueblo *kivas.* Thus on the basis of conventional archaeological reasoning, Hill and Hevly were able to discern three sorts of rooms: habitation, storage, and ceremonial. What did the pollen from these rooms indicate?

Pollen counts from Broken K pueblo were divided into "natural" and "economic" categories, the latter dominated by domestic maize (corn), squash, prickly pear cactus, and other edibles. The economic varieties were assumed to be largely introduced into the deposits by man, while the natural pollen was probably windblown. As expected, the economic pollen was most common in the storage rooms, since stored crops probably dropped their pollen as they were stacked in the room. Habitation and ceremonial rooms had some economic pollen grains but in lower frequencies than the storage rooms. Two kinds of pollen, Mormon tea (*Ephedra*) and buckwheat, were particularly abundant in the ceremonial rooms. It seems likely that since both species are considered sacred by modern Hopi and Zuni Indians, these species served a similar function in prehistoric ceremonies. Although this example is trivial in the sense that we already knew the room functions on the basis of other evidence, the Broken K pollen analysis provides a useful, scientifically valid method for future archaeological research.

## CASE STUDY INTERACTION

I. The Washo lived in two kinds of campsites: permanent village situations and temporary task-specific locations. Since fishing, gathering wild plants, and hunting were the three primary subsistence pursuits of the Washo, a variety of ecofactual debris must have been deposited in their camp middens.

   a. Restricting your attention to Chapters 3 and 4 in *Two Worlds of the Washo*, construct a chart which correlates *all three* subsistence foci with the various campsite types. In the resulting cells of the table, list the specific food resources exploited (physical consequences population), documenting your answers with page references.

EXAMPLE (only partially completed):

| Subsistence Activity | Habitation Sites | | Task-Group Sites |
| --- | --- | --- | --- |
| | *Winter* | *Summer* | |
| *Fishing* | . | native trout (p. 13) | . |
| | . | . | . |
| | . | . | . |
| | | . | |
| *Gathering* | Piñon shells (p. 25) | . | . |
| | . | . | . |
| | . | . | . |
| | . | | |
| | . | | . |
| *Hunting* | . | | . |
| | . | | . |

   b. Ecofacts are obviously not deposited at random since portions of sites are often designated as garbage areas or trash heaps. Some of the ecofactual material is destroyed in the subsistence process, so the remains analyzed by the archaeologist represent a biased and disturbed sample of the original subsistence practices. The Washo, for example, butchered deer near the kill site, bringing only the neck and skull bones back to the campsite. The rest of the deer carcass was submerged in a nearby stream. Such practices must be considered when identifying ecofacts from archaeological sites. What other examples of such differential destruction of ecofacts can you document for the Washo? How would the pollen evidence reflect Washo subsistence, remembering that pollen grains tend to cling to plants carried back to the site? In your discussion, consider both living (habitation) sites and task-specific sites.

II. Although the Huron were a horticulture people, wild plants and animals still provided a significant portion of their overall diet.

   a. What ecofacts would you expect to find in a Huron village which would reflect the true reliance upon hunting, fishing, and collecting of wild plants? Which subsistence activities mentioned by Trigger in *The Huron: Farmers of the North* would you expect to leave *no* traces in the archaeological record? Are these sources significant in the total diet?
   b. How could the archaeologist ascertain the relative importance of horticulture among the Huron? Discuss ecofacts, artifacts, and features. Is there any way to recognize the cornfields of the ancient Huron?

# 5
# Reconstructing Past Lifeways:
## Prehistoric Great Basin Ecology

Traditionally, archaeologists anxious to examine past adaptations have attempted to find deep, stratified sites with a high degree of preservation. Caves and grottos have proven particularly fruitful in this regard. Plant and animal remains have been carefully excavated and analyzed using methods discussed in the last chapter. Recently, however, archaeologists have come to realize the finite nature of their data. Many rivers have been dammed, thereby flooding many of the heavily occupied river bottoms; subdivisions are rapidly encroaching upon wilderness areas where sites have formerly remained untouched; some "amateur" collectors, eager to obtain artifacts and unmindful of scientific purposes, have wantonly destroyed some of the richest sites. Archaeologists are running out of sites. It has been estimated that in California alone over 1000 sites are destroyed annually. While this situation is distressing, the worst is yet to come. It is only a matter of time until archaeologists can no longer strictly rely upon stratified deposits for keys to the past, for all such sites will be gone.

Archaeologists are mindful of this problem and are looking for new avenues of prehistoric research. One relatively untapped resource is the *surface site*, areas in which remains have simply lain on the ground surface rather than becoming buried by sands, silts, and gravels. In areas which have not been extensively plowed, archaeologists have the unparalleled opportunity of collecting artifacts literally where they were dropped, often thousands of years ago.

Not only do those surface areas offer potential laboratories for studying prehistoric remains, but they also represent adaptations different from the more traditionally excavated midden sites. In the past few decades, surface sites have been largely ignored since they lack the contextual relations (stratigraphy) necessary for establishing cultural chronologies. But current archaeology is examining more than merely time-space sequences and surface sites provide unique data regarding past man-land relationships. This chapter considers one such surface area, the Reese River Valley of central Nevada. This project is presented as an illustration of some of the modern techniques which are used to reconstruct past lifeways. Such new directions, while still relatively crude and imperfect, may well chart the thrust of archaeological research in the future. (For further details on the Reese River Ecological Project, the reader is referred to Thomas 1969b, 1972b, 1973.)

## THE GREAT BASIN SHOSHONEANS

The Great Basin is, as the name implies, a massive geographic unit of interior drainage. The few river and stream drainages flow into large "sinks" or playas, so water escapes the Basin only through evaporation. The physiographic boundaries are formed by the Sierra Nevada Mountain range to the west with the Wasatch Mountains flanking the eastern Great Basin. The volcanic Columbian plateau forms the northern margin, which gradually tapers into the arid Mojave and Colorado deserts to the south. As cyclonic storms move eastward from the Pacific Ocean, the Sierras act as a significant topographic barrier, causing the moisture-laden clouds to lose most of their precipitation on the Sierra's western face. The eastern scarp of the Sierras and the Great Basin is therefore relatively arid. This *rainshadow effect* is repeated on a reduced scale throughout the western Great Basin itself so that the comparatively moist west-facing slopes tend to support more verdant stands of trees and shrubs than do the eastern slopes.

The semiarid steppe environment of the Great Basin hosts a varied array of vegetation communities. Often called *lifezones*, these biotic associations provide dramatic contrasts within a relatively small area. In recent times at least, sagebrush is the ubiquitous ground cover, often interspersed with rabbitbrush and wild rose in the more moist areas. A riparian association of cottonwood, aspen, and willow is often so dense near the waterways as to obscure the water itself from view. A thin belt of piñon and juniper trees grows on the numerous mountain ranges. Piñon are replaced at higher elevations by scrubby mountain mahogany, which eventually yield to sagebrush again at the summits. The overall visual effect is of a low, monotonous carpet of sagebrush punctuated by fringes of riparian or montane shrub communities (see Figure 3).

This unique environment fostered an equally distinctive cultural adaptation. Historically, the Great Basin was inhabited by groups of Northern Paiute, Western Shoshone, and Southern Paiute (or Ute), divisions based largely upon linguistic boundaries. The Indians of the Great Basin can be collectively termed the Shoshone-speakers or Shoshoneans, for short. Their ecological adaptation depended upon a meticulous and exacting exploitation of Great Basin *microenvironments*. Since the Shoshoneans practiced no true agriculture, they had to travel from one habitat to another to harvest the local wild crops as they became available. This *seasonal round*, as it is called, required the aboriginal groups to schedule their itinerary in such a way as to fully exploit local productivity. Nuts of the piñon tree, the staple Shoshonean resource, ripened in the late fall and usually provided enough food for the winter. Buffalo berries and currants also became available in the low foothills about this time. Indian rice-grass seeds were usually ripe during the summer months so camp was moved from the piñon forest to the flat valley floor in late spring. Many other local foods were utilized in the same cyclical fashion. Because of their intimate relationship with their natural environment, the Shoshoneans were able to weld isolated native foodstuffs into a solid economic subsistence cycle.

The limits and constraints of the natural environment—what Julian Steward (1938) termed *ecological determinants*—conditioned Shoshonean demography and economy. The vicissitudes of successful adaptation to the Great Basin habitat were reflected also in the social aspects of their lifeway. By its nature, Shoshonean ecology required a sparse, mobile population. The native seed crops could only support between 20 and 30 people in every 100 square miles, and even these small groups moved frequently to new seed areas throughout the year. Large permanent social groupings were impractical and generally impossible to maintain. Only the extended family (*i.e.*, the parents, their unmarried children, and perhaps a grandparent or two) remained in permanent year-round association. Small enough for mobility yet large enough for efficient seed harvesting, these foraging groups (called *family bands*) were the ideal basic unit in the Great Basin ecosystem.

A spirit of pragmatism pervaded the entire Shoshonean social sphere. Marriage was *ad hoc* and primarily an economic affair. Females gathered the seed crops, thereby providing the bulk of the diet. Husbands spent much of their time hunting game, mostly antelope and mountain sheep, to supplement the vegetal diet. The marriage alliance was a brittle one, easily dissolved and reshuffled. Pubescent children married early, with economic provisions overshadowing most other considerations, including romantic inclinations. There was little margin for useless, that is, nonfunctional, cultural norms ("You really should marry your mother's-brother's-eldest-daughter."). What mattered was the creation of an economically viable dyad, suited to surviving the rigors of Great Basin life. No elaborate mortuary practices were observed, for death was accepted as the logical and necessary conclusion to life.

The Shoshoneans, along with the Congo Negritos, the Bushmen, the Eskimo, and the Australians have provided theorists with a cultural baseline from which to reconstruct man's evolutionary cultural blueprint. All of these groups, especially the Basin Shoshoneans, are often cited as representing the minimum possible cultural adaptation. For more basic, simpler social groupings, one must presumably look to the nonhuman primates. Small wonder that in addition to serving as the cultural "baseline," the Shoshoneans have also been important in anthropology as analogies in reconstructing the even more remote adaptation of prehistoric groups, such as the early Pleistocene hunters of Africa.

Yet the Shoshonean adaptation did not remain stable during the historic period. The westward expansion of White settlers in the 1850s drastically altered the Great Basin natural environment. Dense stands of piñon, so critical to the aboriginal lifeway, were timbered by the early silver miners for lumber to shore up the mine shafts and to stoke the furnaces of the voracious stamp mills. Great herds of domestic sheep and cattle—important sources of fresh meat for the settlers—changed the landscape in two ways: Fences had to be built, fostering further lumbering, and the herds were permitted to feed in the Great Basin valleys. The overall effect of overgrazing was devastating to the aboriginal economic system, since the stands of natural grasses, such as wild rye, Indian ricegrass, and *Mentzelia* were destroyed beyond salvation. The prehistoric ecological balance which had been delicately preserved for thousands of years was upset in less than two decades. The piñon groves were reduced to forests of tree stumps and erosion immediately set in. The native grasses, formerly blanketing the valleys in deep green, were replaced by endless sagebrush wastes and imported European grasses, both of which were useless in the aboriginal economy.

It is ironic that the brunt of ecological damage was performed directly by the hand of the Indian himself, who suffered most in the long run. The Shoshoneans were hired by ranchers to herd the livestock and by miners to fell the forests. The advent of wage labor placed the Shoshoneans in the tragic position of undermining their own lifeway. As the mining and ranching industries flourished, more wage labor became available; the environment deteriorated further, and the Indians were forced from aboriginal pursuits into still more wage labor. The Shoshoneans, trapped as they were in this vicious feedback cycle, were the ultimate losers. When the central Nevada silver mines played out in the 1890s, the Indians were forced to return to a quasi-aboriginal economics. But by this time, the ecological situation upon which the Shoshoneans had always depended was so altered that the traditional economic techniques simply did not work anymore.

It was not until the 1930s that anthropologist Julian Steward attempted major ethnographic fieldwork in the central Great Basin. Most Shoshonean informants had been born about 1870, after the initial silver boom. Could these informants, born and enculturated in the midst of such disruptive conditions, be expected to recall the precontact "pristine" lifeway of the Shoshoneans? Some anthropologists, such as Elman Service (1962), think not. Furthermore, some archaeologists feel that Great Basin prehistory does not correlate with Steward's overall interpretation of the historic period (e.g., Cowan 1967, Napton 1969). The primary questions concern the prehistoric Great Basin lifeways. Were the informants questioned in 1930 accurate in their descriptions of precontact conditions, or had acculturation to the Anglo-American invasion significantly changed their ability to relate an accurate description of the past lifeways.

There are several methods of attacking this important question. New ethnographic fieldwork is one such approach, but as Chapter 6 will demonstrate, modern informants could probably shed only limited light on socioeconomic practices which vanished over a century before. An ethnohistoric study of written sources would perhaps be helpful, but the biased accounts of miners, ranchers, and farmers almost invariably distort and deride Indian culture. Furthermore, such sources document only the acculturated period, not the critical prehistoric era. The most workable approach to determine precontact economics and demography is to examine the remains of the prehistoric material culture. That is, the question of prehistoric ecological adjustment can be solved only through carefully planned and executed paleoethnological research; the Reese River Ecological Project was initiated with these express purposes in mind.

## PREREQUISITES FOR ARCHAEOLOGICAL RESEARCH

To be anthropologically relevant, prehistoric data of this sort must satisfy three basic criteria. First, all facets of the seasonal round must be represented, since it is not enough to generalize from a single site. These people moved about from place to place every year, so information from a single cave or rockshelter tells only part of the story.

The data must also be unbiased, because capricious sampling techniques can lead the archaeologist astray in assessing the relative importance of the various hunting/gathering sites. The best scientific way to insure unbiased results in this situation is through judicious use of *random sampling theory*. To conduct such a random sample, one must first choose the sampling *elements* which are the objects of study. In many cases, these elements are archaeological sites in the traditional sense. All of these elements taken together form a set of $N$ possible elements, the sampling *universe*. Each element is assigned a consecutive number from 1 to $N$, and numbers are randomly selected so that each has an equal probability of selection, $1/N$. In this manner, a subset, called the *sample*, of the $N$ elements is chosen, so that each member of the universe has an equal chance of inclusion.

In addition to providing relatively unbiased samples, random procedures have the added benefit of providing data amenable to further statistical manipulation. Since almost all statistical analyses require a random sample, the archaeologist who accepts a biased sampling design immediately and unnecessarily ties his own hands.

Finally, the research design must provide useful *negative evidence*. In addition to telling the archaeologist what activities *did* take place, the data must likewise indicate those activities which *did not* occur in a particular area or lifezone. It is a relatively simple matter, for example, to determine the presence of piñon harvesting sites within the piñon-juniper zone, but the archaeologist should also determine that such sites *do not* also occur (a) near a river, (b) on the sagebrush-covered flatlands, or (c) on the high mountain peaks. The requirement for negative evidence, only recently recognized as relevant to archaeological research, imposes severe yet necessary qualifications upon fieldwork. Only by paying strict attention to the quality of data can archaeologists hope to derive anthropologically viable conclusions.

## RESEARCH DESIGN

The only available research design which can satisfy the above requirements is an *inclusive regional random sample*. The study area (the universe) is selected to include an entire seasonal round. In the central Great Basin, this universe is a single valley system, situated between the north-south trending mountain ranges. The universe is then gridded into a series of large squares (tracts) which are each considered as a sample element. Every tract will be completely searched for all visible remains of prehistoric subsistence activities (sites). In this case, archaeological sites *per se* cannot serve as elements, since prior to survey one does not know how many of what kinds of sites are involved in this particular valley. Finally, the tracts are numbered from 1 to $N$, and a random sample of size $n$ is selected. Economic vicissitudes—time and money available, scope of the project, estimated unit variability, and so forth—determine how many tracts can be selected. The sampling fraction is expressed as $n/N$.

With this generalized strategy in mind, it remains to determine the specific tactics necessary for application in the Great Basin. Such a design assumes that archaeological material will be present on the land surfaces, rather than buried underground. While this assumption is invalid for many geographic areas, the central Nevada region is notable for its relatively stable land surfaces and for its paucity of known buried sites. The tract survey procedure also requires complete cooperation from local landowners, for all possible tracts must be totally accessible to the field teams. Additionally, amateur artifact collecting (*pothunting*) must be minimal so the archaeologist is able to recover reliable samples. Aerial photographs and serviceable access roads are also desirable. A final consideration in selecting an area for research is that the archaeologist who lives where he is working is often able to make observations and gain valuable insights into some of the significant local ecological exigencies. For this reason, most archaeologists prefer to camp near the excavation site or survey area.

## THE REESE RIVER VALLEY

The upper Reese River Valley of central Nevada was chosen as the area best satisfying the prerequisites outlined above. The Reese River is a lazy little stream less than 15 feet wide, which arises about 40 miles south of Austin, Nevada. Flowing northward between the Shoshone and Toiyabe mountain ranges, the Reese finally empties into the Humboldt River. The valley itself is about 15 miles wide and over 100 miles long. For survey purposes, a cross-section was selected to provide a suitable universe which, you will remember, should enclose the area of an annual seasonal round of the historic Shoshoneans. The overall study area comprises a tract of land about 15 miles wide by about 20 miles long.

The valley floor in this area lies about 6500 feet above sea level and is presently dominated by sagebrush shrubs. The piñon-juniper belt, so critical for winter forage, reaches between about 7000 and 8500 feet, covering the low flanks of the mountains. Thick stands of buffalo berries, currants, wild rice, and a host of other native foods also grace the montane forest belt. Above 8500 feet, trees yield again to low sagebrush. The mountain peaks, some of which tower over 11,000 feet, are quite tundralike, practically devoid of vegetation. A riparian zone consisting of willow, aspen, and cottonwood flanks all montane streams, which gradually wind their way toward the Reese River.

These lifezones of the Reese River Valley were clearly defined and easily discerned in the field (see Figure 3). Four lifezones were isolated for study: lower sagebrush-grass, piñon-juniper, upper sagebrush grass, and the riparian zone, including both upland stream margins and the immediate vicinity of the Reese River. This universe was circumscribed on aerial photographs and divided into about 1400 tracts, each of them 500 meters—about one-third mile—on a side. Each tract was numbered and a 10 percent random sample was selected. Each tract is considered as a *sampling element* in this study (see Figure 4).

The actual fieldwork consisted of locating each of the 140 tracts on the ground and then surveying the entire 500 meter square for signs of prehistoric occupation. All artifacts and waste chippage, whether an isolated find or part of a dense concentration, was mapped, cataloged, and collected. The most efficient survey unit was a team of six archaeologists, primarily instructors and students from the Universities of California and Nevada. Each crew could survey between one and one-half and two such tracts daily, depending upon accessibility and local terrain. This random sampling design attempted to minimize bias by forcing archaeologists to look in *every* topographic locale, even those unlikely to have habitation residue. It is not

*Figure 3. Vegetation of the Reese River Valley. Especially note the riparian asso-ciation in the foreground and the piñon-juniper belt on the Shoshone Mountains in the background.*

enough to say that people could not have possibly lived in a particular situation, for such statements are highly colored by the archaeologist's preconceived ideas and are thus unacceptable in scientific research. The random survey established (within statistical sampling error) precisely which localities were or were not occupied, with little bias or ethnocentrism involved. Artifacts recovered were then analyzed by lifezone to determine prehistoric man-land relations.

*A Word about Temporal Controls*

Since the Reese River project is presented as a methodological example of recon-structing an extinct lifeway, a word is in order regarding how such projects control the temporal variable. Unfortunately for the archaeologist, the Great Basic Sho-shoneans and their prehistoric counterparts rarely manufactured pottery, so we are denied this valuable chronological indicator and must look elsewhere in the artifactual repertory for suitable time-markers. The best single category of artifacts in this area is projectile points, the stone tips of arrows, darts, and spears. These artifacts, generally manufactured of a fine-grained silicious stone, are fashioned into shapes suitable for hafting. The shapes change systematically through time and are thus excellent candidates for temporal types. The best way to establish the types and their time ranges is through the excavation of stratified archaeological sites; previous excavations in the central Nevada region have exposed the temporal types, which have now been adequately confirmed by dozens of radiocarbon dates. Stylistic phases have been defined on the basis of these temporally significant artifact types. Let me again underscore the fact that *time controls must be established prior to the attempt to study lifeways.* Any archaeological study lacking control of the

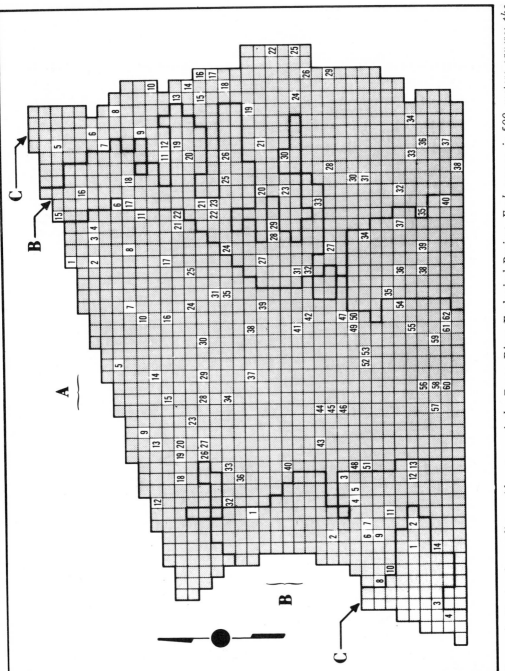

Figure 4. Regional sampling grid system of the Reese River Ecological Project. Each square is 500 meters square; the numbered tracts were selected as the 10 percent random sample (photograph reproduced courtesy Methuen & Co., Ltd.)

temporal dimension recreates only an isolated shred of culture, floating in time and devoid of anthropological significance.

Artifacts recovered in the Reese River survey ranged in time from the historic period back to about 2500 B.C. Four stylistic phases have been discovered: Devils Gate, Reveille, Underdown, and Yankee Blade. The precision of temporal controls is relative, of course, and for our present purposes these four phases can be pooled into a single temporal period, called the Medithermal. For other purposes we might wish to divide the period into its component phases, but the larger period suffices in this context.

*Analysis*

The Reese River fieldwork took about four months to complete with a field crew varying in size from 23 to 45 people. Approximately 3500 artifacts were recovered from the surface of the 140 tracts. As expected, no stratified sites were located in the study area, confirming the assumption of relative geomorphic stability. About a dozen attributes were measured on each artifact and then an IBM card was prepared for each specimen. Artifacts were then analyzed and classified by a computer, in this case a Burroughs 5500. The initial computer output was in terms of *temporal types*, which ranged from roughly 2500 B.C. to historic times. After the temporal range of the samples had been determined, the temporal categories were collapsed in favor of more useful *functional types*, divisions based upon distinctive attribute modes such as cutting edge angle, degree of blade curvature, and others (for the details of the computer work, see Thomas 1971b, 1972b, 1973).

The primary aim of analysis was to establish consistent artifact tool kits which corresponded with the prehistoric exploitation of the lifezones. Areas of extensive hunting, for example, were expected to exhibit a rather distinctive and male-oriented artifact assemblage: spent projectile points, butchering tools (with edge angles generally sharper than about 45°), and flaking debris resulting from resharpening rather than from primary artifact manufacture. Habitation areas, on the other hand, ought to reflect both male and female tasks such as tool manufacture, clothing preparation and repair, remains of cooking activities, house foundations, campfires, ritual paraphernalia, and so on. As with the analytical phase, the computer participated in predicting theoretical artifact distributions (see Thomas 1971b, 1972b). Given all of the proper ethnographic input, such as the activity sequences and the tool kits involved, the computer predicted the relative frequency of each artifact within each lifezone. These predictions were actually the artifact distributions which could be expected from Julian Steward's model of Great Basin subsistence patterns. The primary object of the fieldwork at Reese River was to confirm or reject those theoretical predictions and, by implication, the overall Steward model. The project, in a sense, was testing anthropological theory through the use of archaeological data.

*Results of the Reese River Ecological Project*

The fieldwork and laboratory analysis resulted in an overall synthesis of the archaeology of the Reese River Valley. The pattern of local cultural ecology can be described as a "subsistence-settlement system." That is, the results depict an ecological adaptation which lasted during the Medithermal period, dating from 2500 B.C. to the historic era in the Great Basin. In a strict sense, the Reese River ecological pattern holds only for the Reese River locality, but further research will probably indicate that similar patterns exist throughout much of the central Great Basin.

The Reese River subsistence-settlement system can be characterized by two types of settlements. The *Shoreline Settlement* consisted of a series of large sites located on permanent water sources within the lower sagebrush-grass zones. The artifact assemblage indicates that economic focus was upon the wild grass and root crops which ripen in the late spring and early summer. The shoreline settlements consisted of massive linear scatters of artifacts—often a couple of miles long—which lay parallel to the source of the flowing water. In this context, the "site" was anywhere along the river or stream, for apparently no specific village area was consistently reoccupied. These campsites were probably situated near scattered caches of harvested summer seeds. The only structures were probably brush windbreaks and sunshades. The excessive waste chippage encountered indicates that most of the stone tool manufacture took place in the summer camps. The seed diet was doubtless supplemented by rodents and rabbits, both of which could be easily hunted on the nearby flats.

The other primary focus of habitation, the *Piñon Ecotone Settlement*, was located in the dense stands of piñon and juniper trees, generally on long, low ridges which finger onto the valley floor. This "edge effect," as it is called, is a rather common form of ecological adaptation which allows exploitation of dual lifezones: in this case, both the piñon belt and the nearby valley floor. These sites are also linear scatters of artifacts and chippage, but unlike the shoreline settlements, the piñon ecotone sites consisted of more densely concentrated artifact clusters. There are only a limited number of suitable flat-topped ridges in the area, so the potential areas of habitation were more limited than those along the river. The piñon sites were occupied just after the fall pine cone harvest, so the villages could be established only when the nut crop of the immediate area was successful. In other years, the winter village had to be relocated in some more distant portion of the forest where the piñon nuts were available. The artifact inventory of these sites indicates that most of the hide preparation and clothing manufacture took place during the winter encampments. Deer and mountain sheep probably supplemented the diet of piñon nuts. Houses consisted of domed wickiups, sometimes surrounded by stone circles and covered with piñon tree bark or juniper boughs. These houses were often placed in a shallow pit up to 18 inches deep. Although only about five families could live on each ridge top, there might be several such villages within a one mile radius.

In addition to the habitation sites, the remains of several special-purpose sites were located and mapped. On the flat valley floor, several butchering assemblages were recovered (knives, scrapers, and resharpening flakes), presumably resulting from communal hunting of both jackrabbits and antelopes. Scattered about in the same area were additional artifacts (seed knives and grinding stones) which resulted from women's seed gathering forays. Evidence was also recovered which suggests that deer and mountain sheep were hunted in the piñon belt and also in the high, more barren mountains which flank the Reese River. All of these *task group assemblages* represent short-term, ancillary subsistence activities undertaken by small groups of relatives, working out of the more permanent habitation sites.

In the main, the Reese River subsistence-settlement system can be characterized as a central-based wandering pattern, defined by Beardsley (1956:138) as a

> . . . community that spends part of each year wandering and the rest at the settle-
> ment or "central base," to which it may or may not consistently return in
> subsequent years . . . a half-sedentary community (which) represents an adjust-
> ment to . . . a storable or preservable wild food harvest such as acorn or
> mesquite beans. . . .

The Reese River system can be more properly considered a *dual central-based wandering pattern* since *two* storable foods are involved: piñon nuts and wild seeds. Each crop dictated a distinct area of habitation which was an "on the fence" compromise between wandering and sedentary life. This lifeway provided the flexibility required to succeed in the harsh, unstable Great Basin environment.

*Implications*

This rather extended example has been presented as a case study indicating precisely how archaeology attempts to reconstruct an extinct lifeway. The initial step was to establish a local cultural chronology and then to impose the chrono-logical controls necessary for further investigation. Some rather specific research objectives were then outlined and an archaeological strategy framed to gather the relevant data. In the Reese River case, the more conventional approach of excavating a few large stratified sites would not answer the questions under consideration. A new research design based upon the systematic random sampling of an entire valley was therefore devised to suit the problem at hand. As archaeological research progresses in its anthropological endeavors, the archaeologist will have to adopt more and more nontraditional techniques. It appears that anthropological viability is replacing methodological conformity in archaeology.

Finally, let us tally the overall anthropological significance of the Reese River Ecological Project. First of all, the survey determined the temporal parameters of the area. The Reese River Valley was not significantly occupied prior to about 2500 B.C. Ancillary studies indicate that the vicinity was either too hot or too arid (or both) before this date for a successful human adaptation. Secondly, the project successfully reconstructed the aboriginal seasonal round of the prehistoric Indians of Reese River. Their seasonal round, based as it was upon piñon pine nuts and Indian ricegrass, permitted a flexible and enduring man-land relationship. The overall adaptation hedged against short-term environmental fluctuations because the seasonal round depended upon several crops, not upon a single food resource. There appears to be no significant subsistence change from about 2500 B.C to ethnographic times.

This demographic pattern can now be compared to similar data from any other group, historic or prehistoric. If anthropology seeks to understand the mechanisms of human ecology—man's interplay with nature—then the focus must not be restricted to those social groups which survived into the ethnographic present. Extinct, unsuccessful cultural adaptations must be as carefully studied and documented.

The Reese River project, like most scientific endeavors, posed many more questions than it answered. We are still ignorant about the precise physical relationships between the historic Great Basin Shoshoneans and the prehistoric inhabitants of the Reese River Valley. Perhaps the earliest Reese River people were the prehistoric Shoshone themselves or perhaps the Shoshone were rather late interlopers into this ecosystem, replacing some earlier social group. Furthermore, although the entire 4500 year period has been presented as a unified, stable ecological adaptation, there were clearly some short-term, phase-level subsistence fluctuations which have been glossed over through this holistic approach. Also, the prehistoric ecological relationship of the Reese River Valley to surrounding areas in the central Great Basin is largely unknown. We must admit the unlikely possibility that the Reese River was a veritable Garden of Eden, located in the midst of areas of more meager cultural adaptations. Only further research along the same lines will outline the overall regional patterns.

Probably the greatest gap in our knowledge of the Shoshoneans and their predecessors is with regard to their social structure. Steward (1970:129) has repeatedly stated that the basic social unit of the historic Shoshoneans was the "family band" or "family cluster," discussed earlier. Now it is quite reasonable to assume that a similar social organization prevailed in prehistoric times, but this view is neither well established nor universally accepted. According to anthropologist Elman Service (1962:73), one of Steward's prime critics, "the ecological argument, it is apparent, is useful when demography alone is under discussion, but there is more to social organization than demography. *Human* social organization is cultural." Archaeology is well suited to problems concerning technology and ecology, but the fine nuances of primitive social organization, such as sodalities, statuses, and band structures in general, have had the annoying habit of eluding the archaeologist's most probing shovel. Even at the ethnographic level, these questions are rather poorly understood. The future success (or failure) of prehistoric anthropology to grapple with social correlates of ecological behavior will largely determine and condition the extent of archaeology's contribution to the search for universals of mankind.

## CASE STUDY INTERACTION

I. Since the Washo are hunter-gatherer peoples like the Shoshone and their neighbors, they must move their camp several times during each year, their settlement pattern consisting of diverse types of camps (winter villages, hunting camps, etc.). To the archaeologist reconstructing such movements centuries after the fact, these various site types must be integrated into a coherent prehistoric pattern.

  a. Using materials from *Two Worlds of the Washo*, prepare a settlement pattern chart, listing the following:
     1. Each season of the year across the top.
     2. Settlement pattern variables (see below) down the left side.
     3. Complete each box with data from the Washo settlement pattern.

EXAMPLE (only partially completed):

SPRING

|  | Male | Female |
|---|---|---|
| *Subsistence activities* | Fishing with harpoons<br>•<br>• | •<br>•<br>• |
| *Environmental setting* | Move base camp to Lake Tahoe | |
| *Type of housing* | Caves | |
| *Specialized religious practices* | | |

b. From your subsistence chart, prepare a generalized sketch map showing the movement of a single Washo group throughout a typical year. Be certain to include the following features:
1. Habitation and task group areas (distinguish between two)
2. Permanent topographic features such as hypothetical (or real) lakes, rivers, mountains, desert regions, etc.
3. Natural lifezones
4. Scale in miles

II. Unlike the Washo, the Huron led a sedentary existence—due largely to their agricultural productivity—and they relocated their villages only every 10 or 20 years.

a. Concentrating upon data from Chapters 2 and 3 in *The Huron: Farmers of the North*, construct a rough scale map of a Huron settlement, as it would appear to an archaeologist excavating 500 years after abandonment. Using symbols, draw the expected artifact concentrations throughout the village; on a separate page, be sure to explain each symbol.
b. What special-purpose, nonhabitation sites would you expect to find in Huronia? List the activities involved, the associated topography and artifacts of the physical finds population.

# 6

# Action Archaeology

Scientists studying the past do not always work with the dead. Sometimes archaeologists turn to living peoples for clues in interpreting prehistoric remains. Although these living people are not *data* in the strict sense, the insight of an individual *participating in* a primitive culture can often open the eyes of a modern archaeologist who is trying to discover meaning in artifacts of the past. Richard Gould, an archaeologist now with the University of Hawaii, spent months with the aborigines of Australia and the Tolowa of northwestern California in search of answers to questions arising from his excavations. Why, he quizzed them, did they make their arrowheads in such peculiar, yet regularized, forms? How could they make a living without agriculture or industry? Who lived with whom, and what did their houses look like 100 or 1000 years ago? At one point, Gould asked his Tolowa informants to inspect his excavations so that he could get their ideas on some puzzling artifact types. In order to know where to dig, Gould had looked for concentrations of broken artifacts and midden deposit. He was somewhat chagrined when after repeated digging, he was unable to locate any prehistoric house remains and he asked his informants about the problem. They were quite amused, telling him that ". . . them old-timers never put their houses in the *garbage dump* . . . they don't like to live in their garbage any more than you would!" (Gould 1966:43). They pointed to a steep slope on the edge of the "site." Although this hillside seemed to Gould an unlikely place to build a house, he followed their suggestions. After only 20 minutes of digging, he came upon a beautiful redwood plank house lying only 18 inches under the surface. Gould's Tolowa informants just grinned knowingly.

This kind of fieldwork—termed "action archaeology" by Kleindienst and Watson (1956)—has become an important aspect of modern archaeological research, especially as industrial societies encroach upon lands and customs of the few remaining primitive peoples.

Perhaps the earliest case of action archaeology can be traced back to the research of Dr. Saxton Pope in a touching episode of early anthropology. In 1911, a beaten and defeated Indian (later named "Ishi") was found crouching in a slaughter house corral near Oroville, California. His family had either been murdered or had starved, and Ishi himself no longer had the will to live; he was willing to succumb. Obligingly, the local sheriff locked him in the jail, since "wild" Indians were not to be allowed to roam about in those days. Through good fortune, a young anthropologist at the University of California named Alfred Kroeber learned of Ishi's plight and arranged for his release. Kroeber brought Ishi to San Francisco where he secured quarters for him in the University Museum. From that time until Ishi's death in 1916, Kroeber and his staff taught the Yahi Indian the ways of civilization, while the Indian exchanged his secrets for survival in the wilds of backland California. Clearly Ishi had more to offer. During his stay Ishi developed a hacking tubercular cough—the malady which later cost him his life—and he was treated daily by Dr. Pope, a surgeon from the nearby University of California Medical Center. Over their short association, Pope and Ishi found common ground in their interest in archery. What an odd combination they must have been: the urbane scholar Pope paired with the Yahi Indian, whose hair was singed in tribal custom, shooting arrows in the downtown parks of San Francisco. Pope wrote a book after Ishi's death about his newly found interest in archery, its techniques and strategy. *Hunting with the Bow and Arrow* was published in 1923 and quickly became the bible of the bow-hunting fraternity. Apparently many urbanites were intrigued by such an unusual avocation, and now archery is a big business. This episode is but a single example of how primitive survival arts can be salvaged by students of culture.

Unlike archery, many prehistoric techniques have perished with their practitioners, and archaeology has been forced to attempt to rediscover them. Often called "experimental archaeology," this branch of science is conducted by some of the better-coordinated anthropologists, many of whom have become quite competent at "primitive" skills, such as the manufacture of stone tools. Flint knapping is a messy business and, as a result, archaeological sites are often littered with scores of broken stone artifacts and waste chippage. For constructing cultural chronologies, the superficial outline of the artifact is often enough to determine temporal types; side-notched points may, for example, be later in one region than the corner-notched varieties. But in aspects other than chronology, it becomes imperative that the archaeologist understand every shred of evidence available. Most aboriginal stone-workers are now dead and with them died the trade secrets which could tell us more about their tools. The study of stoneworking and its socioecological correlates is another example of action archaeology in the service of anthropology.

A few dedicated scientists have spent years experimenting with stone tools. Largely through the trial-and-error efforts of men such as Francois Bordes of France and S. A. Semenov of the Soviet Union a tremendous amount has been redis- covered about the process of manufacturing stone tools. Some years ago Don Crabtree, now affiliated with the Idaho State University Museum in Pocatello, undertook a series of carefully documented studies to uncover the true nature of prehistoric stoneworking. One of Crabtree's projects was to discover what techniques were necessary to replicate the *Folsom spear points* discovered at the Lindenmeier site in Colorado. Folsom points, surely some of the world's most exquisite stone artifacts, were originally made between 9000 and 11,000 years ago. These artifacts were probably tied upon spearshafts and used to hunt extinct forms of American bison. Although the stone points are only about 2 inches long, Crabtree counted over 150 minute sharpening flakes removed from their surface (see Figure 5). The most distinctive property of Folsom artifacts is the *flute* or channel flake removed from each side, the purpose of which is unclear. Some archaeologists suggest that these flakes were removed to facilitate hafting to the spearshaft, while other scholars maintain the groove allowed for more rapid release of blood, like "blood grooves" on many modern bayonets. Another possibility is that the flute simply reduced the weight of the stone point, making it a better projectile. At any rate, Crabtree insisted on finding out exactly how such flutes could be duplicated.

Interested in flint knapping for most of his life, Crabtree began his work on the Folsom problem shortly after the Folsom complex was initially documented in 1926. The technical quality and intrinsic beauty of the Folsom point intrigued him, for while most arrowheads can be fashioned in a matter of a few minutes, the Folsoms required hours, assuming that one understood the elusive technique in the first place. In an experimental period lasting over 40 years, Crabtree tried every conceivable method of making the Folsom points. In his final report on his experiments, Crabtree (1966) described 11 different methods of trying to remove such flakes. Most of the methods proved unsuccessful. Either the technique was impossible with primitive tools or the flute removed was too dissimilar to those on the Folsoms. One method in fact only succeeded in driving a copper punch through Crabtree's left hand! The conclusion was that there were only two realistic methods of removing such a flake from an artifact. The first way is to place an antler shaft on the bottom of the unfinished artifact and then strike this punch with a sharp hammer blow. Because of the critical placement of the antler punch, this technique requires two workers. Further investigation led Crabtree to an historic source which described aboriginal American Indian flintworking techniques. Particularly interesting were the observations of a Spanish Franciscan friar, Juan de Torquemada, who travelled among the Central American jungles in 1615.

> They take a stick with both hands, and set well home against the edge of the front of the stone, which also is cut smooth in that part; and they press it against their brest (*sic*), and with the force of the pressure there flies off a knife. . . . Then they sharpen it [the tip of the crutch] on a stone using a hone to give it a very fine edge; and in a very short time these workmen will make more than twenty knives in the aforesaid manner (quoted in Crabtree 1968:449).

Although Torquemada was describing removal of flakes from a polyhedral core, Crabtree thought the method might possibly produce similar results to those evident on the Folsom artifacts. Following Torquemada's descriptions, Crabtree manufactured a chest crutch, padding one end to avoid painful chest injuries and equipping the other end with a sharp antler flaker. An unfinished Folsom point was tied tightly in a vise of wood and thong, and then gripped between the feet of the flint knapper. Using this crutch braced against the chest, fluting flakes were driven off between the feet. The resulting artifacts were practically identical to the Lindenmeier Folson points. Figure 5 illustrates several of the Folsom specimens manufactured by Don Crabtree in this manner.

Although the archaeologist can never be certain that this was the precise method employed over 10,000 years ago, Crabtree's experiments (plus the 250-year-old description by a Spanish friar) give the archaeologist a firmer foundation upon which to base hypotheses. Scientists such as Crabtree have contributed a great deal to our knowledge of the tools of the past. It is important to learn all that they have to tell us, since tools are all that we have from many vanished cultures.

But the experimental approach is but a single facet of action archaeology. Although enlightening about physical techniques, such experiments leave unanswered our questions about social and idiosyncratic implications of prehistoric material culture. Do distinctive social groupings, such as villages or bands, manufacture their tools in characteristic ways? How do group norms condition the

*Figure 5. Folsom points manufactured by Don Crabtree. Note the two "fluting" flakes which were removed from the bottom two specimens (photograph courtesy Don Crabtree and the Idaho State University Museum).*

finished artifact? Do primitive artisans tend to think—like archaeologists—in terms of *artifact types*? Are individual preferences expressed in stone tool assemblages? Questions such as these can never be answered by an experimental approach since the problems require informants who have learned the techniques of stoneworking *within their native cultural matrix*. Experimentation cannot tell us how primitive people think about their artifacts.

To be sure, native stoneworkers are rare in this modern world. Yet such groups do exist, and archaeologists are beginning to recognize their potential contribution to knowledge. We shall disregard for the moment the fine line separating archaeological research and that of cultural anthropology to consider how action archaeology investigates the social correlates of stone tool manufacture.

It was in 1964, as a graduate student at the Australian National University, that J. Peter White first visited the Highlands of New Guinea. Although he worked primarily as a field archaeologist—his doctoral dissertation was the first ever written on the prehistory of New Guinea—White was delighted to find that the local residents still manufactured tools of stone. Realizing the scientific potential of this situation, White framed a research strategy and returned to New Guinea in 1967 to study this vanishing craft, its social implications and correlates (for more details on this project, the reader is referred to White and Thomas 1972).

The informants in his study, the Duna-speakers of the western Highlands of New Guinea, subsist primarily upon domestic pigs and sweet potatoes, which they cultivate in small well-tended gardens. The Duna live in social groups called *phratries*, loosely structured communities numbering between 100 and 1000. They experienced initial contact with European technology less than two decades ago. Although preferring to use steel axes and knives, the adult males were raised by their parents with a complete knowledge of stone tool manufacture and repair. Until just a few years ago, one either made tools of stone or did without.

When a Duna begins to make his tools, he must first collect the proper raw materials. In this case, chert nodules are selected from a nearby stream. Sharp stone chips are then fractured from the raw nodule, called by archaeologists a *core*. There are basically two ways to accomplish this fracturing. The most direct means is by holding the nodule in one hand and then striking it with another rock, in a direct percussion technique. Alternatively, one may exert more control by placing the core upon a large platform stone, called an *anvil*. Using a stone hammer, the core is then smashed into dozens of sharp flakes (see Figure 6). The large amount of lithic debris created in this process is precisely the same sort of garbage which accumulates in most archaeological sites. Sometimes the remains can range over thousands of years. The core is occasionally wrapped in bark so that the resulting flakes tend to be longer and narrower, that is, they are more "bladelike." The bark wrapping also keeps the stone chips and waste flakes from scattering about upon impact.

After observing this process for some time, White questioned the Duna about the kinds of artifacts they were making. In Duna no linguistic distinction is made between the initial core and the flakes driven from it: both are called *aré*. These sharp little tools are used in wood carving, stripping fibers, drilling shells, and shaving ochers into powder for paint. Figure 7 shows one such *aré* used in carving

*Figure 6. Aluni clansman fracturing flakes from a chert core (photograph courtesy of J. Peter White).*

barbs upon a Duna hunting spear. Although steel knives hold a better edge, completely adequate work can be accomplished with the lithic counterpart.

Some flakes are selected for a more specialized function. These flake tools, called *aré kou* by the Duna, are tied with orchid fibers into the handle of cane or wood, and then are used for drilling holes or shredding fibers. To the archaeologist, the Duna distinguish two types that are distinct in morphology, function, and cognitive significance. To the Duna, the archaeologist has made a lot of fuss about nothing. These are simply old-fashioned tools which nobody bothers to make anymore. But archaeologists are somewhat accustomed to being scoffed at for their unusual interests in the garbage of others.

In planning his research among the Duna, White elected to examine some previously unexplored social correlates of artifact manufacture. Specifically, given an assemblage of similar stone tools, what can one tell regarding the cultural matrix in which they were manufactured? In other words, what are the variables of flint knapping? Technological aspects of stone toolmaking—method of flaking, selection of flakes for hafting, and so forth—are somehow related to functional variables and to differences in raw material. These in turn ought to be observable in the local tool traditions in the villages. Individual variation also affects the final appearance of the tools. In order to study these aspects in an objective manner, a research design was formed which held all variables constant save the one under immediate study.

The first such variable concerned fluctuation of tool morphology in artifacts

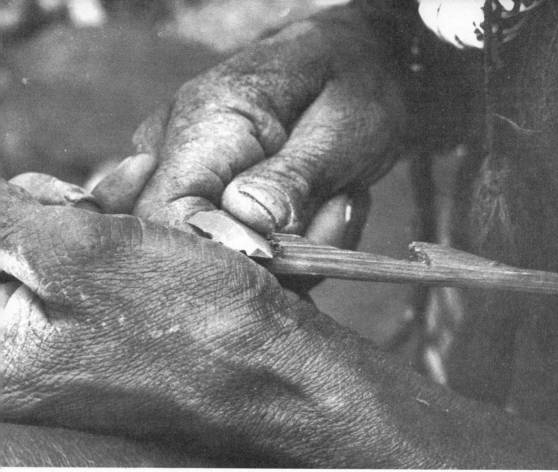

*Figure 7.* Aré *being used to carve barbs into a wooden arrowhead (photograph courtesy of J. Peter White).*

manufactured by the same worker. Making crude stone tools like this involves an element of randomness, reflecting both the haphazard nature of stone fracture and the range of tolerance for acceptable tools. Perhaps these tolerances vary from day to day, even within the same worker. Once this variation per individual can be properly isolated, these figures can serve as a baseline against which to compare other independent variables. Another source of patterned variation is that between workers, since some men are likely to be more consistent in their artifact manufacture, or perhaps more skilled in the mechanics of flaking stone. There could also be differences between the local phratries, since daily face-to-face contact could be expected to condition group norms for tool manufacture. What is a satisfactory tool to one group might seem "odd" or "sloppy" to its neighbors.

In all, three independent variables were isolated in the stone tool complex of the Duna: functional differences, idiosyncratic variations, and group normative patterns. White's project attempted to determine which, if any, of these dimensions of variability could be detected in the stone tools. If patterns could be isolated in the ethnographic sample, collected under strict control, then similar forms of variability could be postulated for (prehistoric) assemblages where such external controls are lacking. This study could also provide anthropological data regarding the contemporary culture of the Duna, especially the articulations between material culture and their systems of norms (mental templates). Once again, the operational boundary between archaeology and anthropology becomes a fuzzy one.

Two phratries were selected for study. *Hareke*, a dispersed grouping of about 375 people, is situated about 15 miles—a five-hour walk—from *Aluni*, a smaller community with only 160. White initiated his project by observing the overall range of techniques used by the Duna in artifact manufacture. After he understood the basics of Duna technology, he asked several knappers in each phratry to prepare batches of tools for him. Eighteen men were selected as informants, ten from Hareke and eight from Aluni. Every day, these men produced between 20 and 75 individual tools, of both *aré* and *aré kou* types. Each individual's daily output was cataloged as a unit, so the basic element of analysis was a single worker's daily output for each tool type. This analytic unit was termed a *TMD*, a "type-man-day." In this manner, tools could be analytically separated in the laboratory. Stoneworker output could be sorted by maker to study individual bias, by daily output to examine the worker's variations from day to day, and also by village to study the relationship of tool traditions in each phratry. Through such reasoning, White constructed a research design in which the three variables under analysis—variation between types, variation between individuals, and variation between villages—could be held constant relative to other sources.

After a couple of months, over 9000 artifacts had been procured in this experiment and the problem became how to effectively analyze such a bulk of data. The first step was to measure individual attributes which seemed to best reflect variation in each assemblage (TMD). One is limited in quantitative analysis of these rather amorphous flakes since there are only a few measurable variables (see Figure 7). White selected six attributes which the Duna themselves felt were important: length, width, thickness, edge angle, weight, and length/width ratio. The informants, of course, do not think of their tools in terms of measurable attributes, but they do have rather strong feelings about what makes a serviceable tool ("It should be *so* long, about this wide, very sharp. . . .").

These measurements resulted in a tremendous mass of data, too much for an individual to handle by pencil-and-paper means, so the aid of a computer was enlisted to handle the tedious analytical operations. Measurements were transferred to IBM cards and processed on a Burroughs 5500 computer at the University of California, Davis. After the machine routinely accomplished the thousands of calculations, it drew graphs to indicate the distributions of each of the attributes. The machine was then directed to further analyze the data by a rather advanced statistical technique shown as "principle component analysis." Although these computations were performed in a matter of minutes by the computer, the task would have taken several trained men their entire lifetimes to perform similar mathematical operations.

The initial conclusions are indicated by statistical testing; without doubt the men of Hareke differ from their Aluni neighbors in standards of tool manufacture. Although both communities consist of a relatively uniform group of individuals (that is, they are of the same *culture*), *aré* and *aré kou* from Hareke are generally longer, wider, thicker, and heavier than those of Aluni. This is significant because workers of both phratries seem to maintain that there is *no* difference between the tools of the two groups. In this simple study, the archaeologist with his measurements and his computer is able to distinguish meaningful size differences of which the actual tool makers are unaware. Further implications of the principal component analysis are even more noteworthy.

In the second step, instead of separating each of the six variables for independent analysis, the attributes were grouped into significant patterns. Length, width, thickness, and weight, for example, are all measurements reflecting a single underlying *supervariable*: size. The analysis determined that as a synthetic abstraction, size contributed almost 70 percent of the total variability in all of the tool measurements. Sharpness (edge angle), on the other hand, was a relatively independent variable, interacting little with size, so edge angle could be considered as an independent supervariable. The computer output listed the following results:

| Supervariable | Initial Measurements | Percent Importance |
|---|---|---|
| Size | Length, width, thickness, weight | 68.7 |
| Width | Width | 16.6 |
| Sharpness | Edge angle | 13.2 |

Total variance accounted for    98.5

This means that considering these three supervariables, one can recreate over 98 percent of the total variation present in the Duna artifact assemblage. It is easy to visualize why size and sharpness are independently involved in such tools, but the fact that width operates independently of size is somewhat surprising. White thinks that this effect is due to the hafting process of *aré kou*. Since the wooden shafts must be about the same size, the potential width of the flakes is severely restricted.

These mathematical results can also be interpreted in terms of more concrete human behavior. Figure 8 represents a small portion of the computer output comparing the work of four of the Aluni men. The vertical dimension is artifact width, while the horizontal axis represents the supervariable, total size. Each numbered point represents a single TMD, a type-man-day. The circled areas represent *aré*, while the uncircled zones depict *aré kou*. Initially, we can easily distinguish between tool types, since *aré kou* are always smaller than *aré*. This is particularly interesting since the informants were unaware of any significant difference between the two types.

Looking at the principal components results from within each community, a second significant pattern which emerges is that technicians seem to have a clear conception of *type*. That is, each man has a *mental template* which directs how his artifacts "should be." Individual number 5 from Aluni—his name is Daka—consistently manufactures his *aré kou* wider than either individual 7 (Agele) or artisan number 8 (Tange). Aluni worker number 6 is less careful in the manufacture of his tools, since he tolerates a wider range of total size, especially in his *aré*. The overall effect is rather analogous to a marksmanship contest. Everyone aims at individual targets, but some men are better sharpshooters than others. The more skilled participants shoot with "tight patterns," closely grouping their consecutive

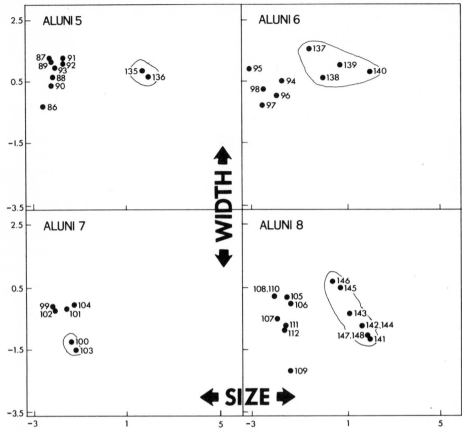

*Figure 8. Computer output from principal component analysis of New Guinea stone tools plotting the supervariables* size *and* width. *The circled area represents* aré *and the uncircled area depicts* aré kou *(modified from White and Thomas {1972} and reproduced courtesy J. Peter White and Methuen & Co., Ltd.).*

shots. Other, less skilled individuals seem to hit all over the target. Although nobody may ever hit the dead center of his target, most marksmen consistently shoot near the bull's eye. This same clustering pattern is apparent in Figure 8. Mental templates are merely sets of slightly differing targets and statistical manipulation of the data is necessary to separate the shot pattern from the actual target at which each contestant aims.

Figure 8 thus provides information about the remaining source of variation, variation within and between workers. In general, people exhibit parallelisms in their artifact classifications. One fellow makes his tools consistently larger, wider, and sharper than a colleague who puts up with more variability in his tools. Instead of aiming at a different target (mental template), the workers are just exhibiting different dispersal patterns in their marksmanship. It is also interesting to note, once again, that although the workers themselves are totally unaware of these differences, the detailed computer analysis leaves no doubt that such differences exist. The observed variations are unquestionably the result of mental templates carried about in the head of each artisan. The informants, however, are ignorant of the existence of such templates.

In looking at the implications of this study, one is first struck with the fact that sociocultural parameters can be accurately defined using metric limits of artifact classes. The size, width, and edge angle supervariables (components) can, almost without exception, separate the 9000 tools by artifact type and by phratry of manufacture. This indicates that two distinctions are implicit in the Duna mental template. Each phratry has established implicit size limits for its two types of tools. *Aré* must be longer than *aré kou*. The larger *aré* are held in the hand while the *aré kou* are more delicate in order to fit into their cane handle. The abrupt boundary in sharpness suggests an equally rigid demarcation in the Duna mental template.

The tools from Hareke are always (in a statistical sense) larger than those from Aluni. Each village made the same tool types for the same functions. However, setting aside differences in raw materials, apparently the Hareke mental template dictates that their tools should be larger than those manufactured at Aluni, but the Duna are unaware of such distinctions. Both metric divisions are significant statistically and indicate that through rigorous quantification of stone tool assemblages, archaeologists should be able to infer functional and/or prehistoric social differences. I do not suggest that these results are universal or that archaeologists can immediately measure a few arrowheads and reconstruct complex paleosocial networks. This study simply validates the disputed premise that socioecological behavior is often coded, as it were, in the stone artifacts and that metric analysis is a proper mechanism with which to decode such evidence.

Peter White's work also tells us something about the archaeological type concept. Previously, some archaeologists have suggested that archaeological classifications should always attempt to mirror mental patterns in the mind of the maker. That is, regardless whether one is dealing with temporal or functional types, this argument holds that these types are *also* cognitive types, corresponding to a prehistoric mental template. The Duna artifacts were formed into discrete types based upon metric attributes, and these preliminary categories did in fact correspond quite well with the natively defined categories, *aré* and *aré kou*. But upon close questioning, the Duna uniformly denied that they recognized this size difference between types. They were also unaware of the differences between the phratries and between individual flint knappers. White's New Guinea experiment suggests that differences between artifact assemblages which are salient for the archaeologist may go unrecognized by the stoneworkers themselves and that people are not necessarily aware of the mental templates which they carry about in their own heads.

One final implication concerns idiosyncratic variation. Stoneworkers, like many artisans and craftsmen, have characteristic methods of performing their craft. While artifacts cannot yet be used to "fingerprint" long-deceased technicians, it is conceivable that further research may disclose that much of the so-called "typological variation" observable in prehistoric assemblages is no more than variation between contemporary craftsmen.

## CASE STUDY INTERACTION

I.  In *Two Worlds of the Washo*, James Downs (p. 50) suggests that Washo social patterns can be understood in terms of the dynamics of their hunting and gathering economy. Since deer hunting provided a significant proportion of the Washo diet, efficiency was a survival necessity. Washo hunters had to cooperate closely in order to secure the wily deer, and therefore it was imperative that males reside in stable groupings and remain in association throughout their life. Friendly boyhood games fostered a cooperative spirit and communal bond early in life, and when a man married he chose a woman from another village but established his new household in his natal community. In this way, the same men resided together for life, while women were "outsiders," imports from other neighborhoods. Many archaeologists, such as James Deetz (1965), have suggested that these residence patterns should be apparent in the artifact assemblages. Men tend to learn to make their tools from their fathers, while women usually learn their skills from their mothers. Continuous face-to-face association implies artifactual stability, while frequent movement and reassociation introduces more random variability into artifact design. In the Washo case, which is patrilocal, each father taught his son, who in turn instructed his son and so on. But young girls learned from their mothers in one camp and then taught their own daughters in the village of their husbands. Since women are always surrounded by strange, unrelated females, their artifacts should tend to be more variable, more random because of these changing influences.

In considering the *total* Washo artifact assemblage—the physical consequences population—discuss at least *eight* discrete functional artifact types which should be expected to exhibit this residence patterning. Identify whether the manufacturer is male or female, and explain specifically which attributes should be involved. Document your statements with page references.

EXAMPLE:    In the precontact Washo society, women taught their daughters to make beautiful coiled basketry from locally available willow branches. The daughters then took up residence with their husbands in new villages, where they taught the granddaughters to manufacture their baskets. Because the mother passes on both techniques from her natal village and those of the husband's village, one can expect considerable variability in the selection of design motifs, colors employed, type of stitch, basket size and shape. Since natural materials had to be collected, environmental resources necessary for basketry would vary between regions, thereby introducing more randomness in basket morphology.

II.  Unlike the Washo, the Huron were matrilocal, with a newly married couple moving into the settlement of the wife's clan. In this case, the females enjoyed technoenvironmental continuity, while the husbands were the outsiders. Perhaps this pattern had something to do with the increased decline in Huron hunting. How would you expect the artifacts to reflect this matrilocal mode of residence? Pick *eight* specific functional artifact types from *The Huron: Farmers of the North*, and discuss precisely which attributes should reflect this residence patterning.

# 7

# The Study of Cultural Processes

Process, as I understand it, refers to the dynamic relationships (causes and effects) operative among components of a system or between systemic components and the environment.

Lewis Binford (1968b)

To many archaeologists, the study of cultural processes is a rather recent phenomenon generally restricted to the past decade or so. But the acknowledged leader of the "processual school" Lewis Binford has clearly stressed his scholarly indebtedness to the earlier work of Gordon Willey (Binford 1962, 1968a:7). In 1958, Willey joined his Harvard colleague Philip Phillips to produce a book entitled *Method and Theory in American Archaeology* in which they suggested that, like all sciences, archaeology operates on three hierarchical levels of organization:

| *General Science* | *Archaeology* |
|---|---|
| Explanation | Processual integration |
| Description | Cultural-historical integration |
| Observation | Fieldwork |

There can be little question that the bulk of archaeology to date has been concerned with the first level of the Willey and Phillips hierarchy: observation. During the deep depression days of the 1930s archaeological fieldwork provided jobs for hundreds of the nation's unemployed, and the artifacts accumulated at an unprecedented rate. Only recently, in fact, have professional archaeologists caught up with the tremendous backlog of data from the WPA days. At the descriptive level, facts are generally integrated into spatial schemes of culture history. Well over half of the Willey-Phillips volume was such a synthesis. But with regard to processual integration, Willey and Phillips were forced to admit that "so little work had been done in American archaeology on the explanatory level that it is difficult to find a name for it. . . ." (1958:5). Despite this lack of progress in the mid-1950s, the Willey and Phillips statement served to focus attention upon the ultimate goal of archaeology. There is no more articulate summary of this position than that offered 15 years ago by Willey and Phillips (1958:2, emphasis added):

Archaeology, in the service of anthropology, concerns itself necessarily with the nature and position of unique events in space and time, but has for its *ultimate purpose the discovery of regularities that are in a sense spaceless and timeless.*

Willey and Phillips pointed the general direction, but it remained for other archaeologists to find the path. The common goal of science is the systematic search for laws, but what are *archaeology's* laws, and how would we recognize one if we stumble upon it? As we shall see, laws are not stumbled upon but rather found only by careful search.

## LAWS

The word "law" is ambiguous because, as it is used in a legal sense, it is a structure that can be broken. Laws of this kind are formal prohibition of acts that people are prone to commit anyway, and can be expected to continue to commit, if on a reduced scale. A law prohibiting jaywalking, for example, suggests the possibility of someone, somewhere actually crossing a street illegally. Why else would we need the law? In sharp contrast to this, scientific laws are inviolable. A law of nature is a statement of what was, what is, and—we have every reason to think— what shall be. A scientific law is no more or less than a complete description of what actually happens under stated conditions. As scientific laws become more fully expressed and completely understood, the better they are able to describe phenomena. To imply that a law of this sort could somehow be violated is absurd, inasmuch as one cannot disobey what actually happens. As philosopher John Kemeny (1959:38) has suggested, the laws of nature do not *prescribe*, they *describe*.

The most interesting aspect of such scientific laws is that they also describe the future. That is, laws enable us to predict events which have not yet occurred. The law of gravity, for example, not only tells us about the behavior of objects which *have fallen* and *are falling*, but also about all objects which *will fall*.

Since the data of archaeology are past events, the question arises as to precisely what the archaeologist wishes to predict. Have not all archaeological events already taken place? Is there such a thing as *predicting the past*? As the title of this book suggests, one *can* predict the events of the past. Lewis Binford (1968b:271) has reminded us that although the archaeological record is comprised of past events, the *knowledge* of this record is a contemporary phenomenon. The Folsom culture discussed today is not the same Folsom culture which was discovered in New Mexico in 1926, although we generalize from some of the same artifacts and features. Scientific archaeology predicts events of the past, but these events are new in the sense that they are *new to us*. Predicting and verifying that a massive drought occurred in 1530 B.C. is no less a scientific achievement than predicting that such an event will occur sometime in the future.

Although all sciences desire to formulate laws of nature, each specific science deals with its own theoretical structures and subject matter. The laws of physics deal primarily with motion; those of chemistry involve molecular reactions; those of social science relate to actions and reactions of *Homo sapiens*. The laws of paleo-ethnology are likewise colored by conditions which are uniquely archaeological-anthropological. These characteristics can best be understood through an illustrative example.

Two threads seem to run through the history of anthropology: Darwin's theory of biological evolution by natural selection and theories regarding the progressive evolution of culture. While modern biology and physical anthropology have provided ample support for Darwinism, the *cultural* evolutionists have lagged far behind. Even today, there are many anthropologists who rebel at the very notion that cultural evolution can be described in lawlike fashion. Part of this disagreement is terminological, since people often use the same words for different ideas. We owe much to Marshall Sahlins and Elman Service for their lucid clarification of this semantic issue. They suggest that cultural evolution is most profitably viewed as a "double-faceted phenomenon."

> Any given system—a species, a culture, or an individual—improves its chances for survival, progresses in the efficiency of energy capture, by increasing its adaptive specialization. This is *specific evolution*. The obverse is directional advance or progress stage by stage, measured in absolute terms rather than by criteria relative to the degree of adaptation to particular environments . . . a man is higher than an armadillo . . . this is *general evolution* (Sahlins and Service 1960:94–95, emphasis added).

The primary distinction is between "cultures" and "Culture." Specific *cultures* adapt to their unique cultural-environmental setting, generally moving toward increasing specialization. *Culture*, on the other hand—the world-wide network of man's societal groupings—is frequently moving from heterogeneity toward homogeneity, as more technologically advanced groups expand over the world at the expense of the less powerful cultures.

With these two types of evolution in mind, we can examine an anthropological law, which Service termed the *Law of Evolutionary Potential*:

> The more specialized and adapted a form in a given evolutionary stage, the smaller its potential for passing to the next stage. Another way of putting it . . . is: Specific evolutionary progress is inversely related to general evolutionary potential (Sahlins and Service 1960:97).

Service's law states that the less well-adapted cultures have more potential for achievement than the specialized groups. The archaeological record abounds with examples of this law (often in the guise of the "northern barbarian" invasion). It strikes many as odd that the Romans, formerly a backward tribal society, were able to surpass classic Greece. But Service's law tells us that this is precisely what one would expect, since at that particular time the Neolithic peoples of Europe had the *greater evolutionary potential*. Mexican prehistory is replete with cases of raiders from the north—Chichimecs—who time after time overwhelmed the established state. Moving from their homeland on the primitive frontiers of northern Mexico, the Toltecs moved south to found Tula, the city-state which ruled after the fall of classic Teotihuacan. Tula later suffered the same fate as Teotihuacan, namely destruction at the hands of another semibarbaric group of Chichimecs. The common denominator is that, all else being equal, rapid evolutionary progress occurs among the have-nots, not among the establishment. Agriculture did not arise, as we shall see, among the hunter-gatherer groups in the favored areas, but rather in areas of stress and competition. Plant domestication appeared initially among those who were not deeply mired in some stable, yet conservative, productive network.

The Law of Evolutionary Potential—indeed, as is true of any cultural law—is thus neither a purely anthropological nor a strictly archaeological artifice: it is both. As archaeological data are progressively incorporated into general anthropological theory, rigid lines will continue to blur and such laws will become an amalgam—archaeological-anthropological laws. Generalizations stated in lawlike fashion will also often be probabilistic in nature. The Sahlins-Service law is one of *potential* not strict determinism. Archaeological laws cannot be expected to be exact since such statements are often about incompletely understood phenomena. That is, we are only dealing with successive approximations of the laws of nature, and we can only hope that such predictions will be correct *most* of the time until we can specify more and more closely the conditions under which the phenomenon will *always* occur! Additionally, all experiments in the real world, especially the archaeological world, are subject to errors in observation and errors in interpretation. Although we have a powerful method for handling errors (the theory of statistics and probability), we can never be 100 percent sure of our facts. Although an experiment may confirm a theory, we can never be absolutely positive that this outcome is not in error. Since the laws of nature are always incompletely known and experiments are always subject to error, archaeological-anthropological laws must often be couched in mediating terms such as "potential," "most likely outcome," "will usually" and "most frequently." The point is that the phenomena are not necessarily uncertain, it is often only the *statement* of the laws which is uncertain.

## THE SCIENTIFIC METHOD

To date, archaeology has experienced only relatively minor success in discovering the complex laws of nature. There are some who claim this is to be expected, since archaeological data are so vague and refractory. Others assert that no such laws exist. The most plausible reason for the relative lack of success in uncovering laws lies in the methods generally employed in archaeology, rather than in its recalcitrant subject matter. If archaeology proclaims itself a science, with the primary goal of discovering laws, then archaeology really ought to follow established scientific procedure, for science is defined more by its method of analysis than by its subject matter.

Let us examine how the scientific method works in archaeology by studying the search for the origins of plant domestication in the New World. In 1948, Herbert Dick, then a graduate student at Harvard University, excavated a site in southwestern New Mexico named Bat Cave. In addition to producing the typical examples of material culture from that area—projectile points, pottery vessels, shell beads, basketry, sandals, and so on—Bat Cave yielded a very primitive form of corn. Radiocarbon tests indicated that these stubby little corncobs were over 4000 years old, making them the oldest and most primitive corn known at that time. Later in the same year, Richard MacNeish discovered similar specimens in the caves of Tamaulipas, not far below the Mexican border. In the next few years, other northern Mexican excavations failed to recover any corn older than about 3000 B.C. In searching for older evidence of plant domestication, MacNeish travelled far to the south into Guatemala and Honduras. Although he found no ancient corncobs, corn pollen was located in strata also dating about 3000 B.C.

With these data to work with, MacNeish paused to plan his next move. Since corn was no older than 3000 B.C. in both North America and far to the south in Central America, MacNeish reasoned that *if* any older corn exists it should be found somewhere *between* the two areas tested, somewhere in southern Mexico. Additionally, intensive genetic studies conducted by MacNeish's colleague Paul Mangelsdorf indicated that corn had probably been domesticated from a highland grass. At this point, MacNeish decided that the best place to look for early domestication was in the arid uplands of southern Mexico.

In order to test this speculative theory, MacNeish made some specific predictions to be tested in the field. Studying maps of southern Mexico, he narrowed his search to a couple of prime targets. The first area examined was Oaxaca, which was investigated and then rejected, for no early corn was to be found there. Then MacNeish moved on to his second choice, the Tehuacan Valley of Puebla State, Mexico. Since corncobs can be expected to survive only in dry deposits, the search was limited to cave sites. After personally examining 38 such caves, MacNeish excavated Coxcatlan Cave, which produced six tiny corncobs more primitive than any ever discovered previously. Subsequent radiocarbon tests placed their antiquity at about 5600 years, a full 500 years older than other corn. Not only did these findings verify MacNeish's theory about the origins of corn in Mexico but they also help us understand the overall processes of man's relationship to domesticated plants and animals. (For a more complete discussion of this work see MacNeish [1964].)

MacNeish's well-reasoned expeditions illustrate three essential components of the scientific method as applied to archaeology: induction, deduction, and verification. MacNeish commenced with a careful assessment of the known facts, the Bat Cave corn, the Tamaulipas finds, the reconnaissance in Guatemala and Honduras, and the available genetic information. Through the process of *induction*, MacNeish formed a theory to explain all of these known facts.

If the facts can be viewed as points on a graph, then induction is like drawing a line to adequately describe these points. In each instance, there are infinite theories which can account for the known facts and the initial task of the scientist is to examine many of the possible theories, eliminating as many as possible. For points on a graph, the most credible line would be the one which passes through each point, regardless of their configuration. If the points tend to fall in linear order, then a straight line would be the *simplest* theory. Throughout the history of science, simplicity has proven the most effective single criterion for selecting between competing theories. When considering the facts, MacNeish doubtless could have come up with any number of theories to explain these facts: corn could have been domesticated simultaneously all over Mesoamerica at 3000 B.C.; corn was domesticated independently in both the north and the south at the same time (3000 B.C.); corn was not domesticated in Mesoamerica at all, but rather traded from somewhere else, such as South America or even Mesopotamia. These are just a few of the large number of possible theories which could be cited to explain the archaeological facts. By choosing the theory he did, MacNeish selected the simplest of the available possibilities. But regardless of which hypothesis is initially selected, no theory can be accepted until it has been successfully tested upon independent data. Mere induction does not lead to scientific acceptance.

Theories—general statements synthesizing facts—cannot be directly tested since one tests only specifics, not generalities. Kemeny (1959:96) notes that "the key to the verification of theories is that you never verify them. What you verify are the logical consequences of the theory." Determining a theory's logical consequences is called *deduction*, the second major step of the scientific method. When MacNeish applied his theory to the map of southern Mexico, he was operating deductively, since the areas selected for potential fieldwork were specific logical consequences of his general theory of domestication.

The final operation of the scientific method is the actual *verification* of the theory upon independent data. In the MacNeish example, verification entailed reconnaissance in archaeologically unknown regions of southern Mexico, illustrating the important point that verification must involve data *independent* from the facts initially studied in the formation of the theory. These new data were analyzed and the theory would have been tentatively rejected had the predictions not been verified. The Tehuacan excavations confirmed MacNeish's theory, so the proposition can be elevated to the status of a lawlike statement. Of course, a single experiment can never completely validate any theory and more intensive investigations are always necessary to increase the credibility of the theory. MacNeish's work at Tehuacan now stands as new data, ready for synthesis into more inclusive theories, which must again be tested in similar fashion. Scientific progress thus consists of the progressive pyramiding of verified theories into a hierarchy of more generalized laws.

## ORIGINS OF OLD WORLD AGRICULTURE

In discussing MacNeish's work on the domestication of maize in Mexico, we had but a short glimpse at one of man's most significant inventions—the development of plant and animal domestication. Through the work of MacNeish and others, it is clear that agriculture was invented at least twice in the evolution of mankind. The Mexican heartland came upon the techniques of domesticating wild plants entirely independent from similar discoveries in the so-called Fertile Crescent of the Near East. If domestication was invented more than once, then one must wonder what causes man to deliberately alter his natural environment. Are there certain circumstances which cause men to automatically domesticate plants and animals? Or did two groups just accidentally stumble across the genetic principles which allow the exploitation of a radically new food source? In short, what are the *underlying processes* involved when man decides to *create* his own food resources?

The study of processes involved in plant domestication is a multifaceted field. MacNeish applied the scientific method in tracking down some of the clues in Mexico; Lewis Binford has also called upon established scientific procedures to explore early plant domestication in the Near East. In Binford's work (1968c) we can see a most sophisticated example of archaeology's third and primary goal, elucidating cultural processes.

Archaeologists have speculated about the origins of European agriculture for almost a century (see Wright 1971 for an excellent review of this problem). Quite early, it became clear that at least two distinct lifeways operated in prehistoric

Europe. The older method centering about hunting large game animals and collecting wild plant foods not unlike the Shoshone (Chapter 5) and the Washo in prehistoric North America. Prehistorians refer to this hunting-gathering stage as *Paleolithic* or the "Old Stone Age." A second way of life evolved when man directly interfered with nature in order to obtain more abundant food sources. This interference involved the selective breeding of plants and animals in the era known as *Neolithic*, the "New Stone Age."

Both Paleolithic and Neolithic lifeways were recognized during Darwin's time, but more recent scientific interest has gradually turned to consider the *interface* of the two Stone Ages—how man evolved from forager to farmer. Some scholars felt that Europe was abandoned during this period, while others now recognize a third transition phase, the *Mesolithic* (see Binford 1968c:313–315). As more coastal and riverine sites were explored, the framework of a "Middle Stone Age" lifeway became apparent as a time of extensive exploitation of marine and aquatic resources. Ecological studies such as those described in Chapter 4 indicate that as the glaciers retreated to expose the mainland, the Mesolithic lifeway began to flourish. The precise relationship between the environmental shifts and the simultaneous change in ecological adaptation is critical in our understanding of the origins of plant domestication.

Countless theories have been advanced to explain man's initial efforts at domestication. One of the more important of these explanations, termed the "oasis theory," was championed by the British archaeologist V. Gordon Childe. Briefly stated, Childe's theory held that as the Pleistocene ("Ice Age") glaciers melted, the world's climate became warmer and generally more arid. In the desert areas, especially those of the Near East, acquisition of water became a major problem for survival. As both men and animals flocked to the oases and exotic desert streams in the difficult search for nourishment, the forced association between man and beast eventually produced a symbiotic relationship. In time, this situation grew from mutual benefit to mutual dependence. The mechanism for the beginnings of animal domestication has been explained in rather simple terms by Childe (1951: 68–69):

> The huntsman and his prey thus find themselves united in an effort to circumvent the dreadful power of drought. But if the hunter is also a cultivator, he will have something to offer the famished beasts: the stubble of his freshly reaped fields will afford the best grazing in the oasis. Once the grains are garnered, the cultivator can tolerate half-starved mouflons or wild oxen trespassing upon his garden plots. Such will be too weak to run away, too thin to be worth killing for food. Instead, man can study their habits, drive off the lions and wolves that would prey upon them, and perhaps offer them some surplus grains from his stores. The beasts, for their part, will grow tame and accustomed to man's proximity.

The domestication of animals was possible in Childe's scheme only after man has become a successful cultivator of plants. In order to find the roots of floral domestication, one needed to look only so far as the nearby Nile Valley. The "nobler grasses"—ancient ancestors of modern wheat and barley—apparently grew in abundance on the banks of the Nile, where they were subjected to annual flooding and enrichment by the rich alluvial soil. Childe felt that plants of the Nile Valley were controlled by nature's perfect irrigation cycle, and that it remained only for "some genius" to artificially produce similar irrigation conditions elsewhere.

While Childe and others felt that the Egyptian area held the key to early domestication, a second competing hypothesis—called by Wright (1971:455) the "Natural Habitat Zone Model"—was proposed by Harold Peake and H. J. Fleure (1927). The Peake-Fleure proposal focussed upon a number of preconditions which they felt were critical in the origin of domestication:

1. The natural area must have hosted a regular and reliable harvest each year.
2. The geography must have been rather restricting so that man was required to stay put and change rather than simply move elsewhere with his old adaptation.
3. The area could not have been forested or swampy, since early technology did not allow for clearing of forests or filling of swamps.
4. The area could not have been isolated, for contact with other cultures was necessary to facilitate the breakdown of custom and taboo which could have inhibited change.

After considering a number of candidates, Peake and Fleure felt that only Southwest Asia measured up. Especially critical was the natural distribution of wild plants (particularly wild wheat, emmer, and einkorn) for domestication, and also wild cattle and goats. The Peake-Fleure argument held that climatic change precipitated domestication of plants and animals only in the areas of their natural occurrence.

Shortly after World War II, Robert Braidwood of the University of Chicago travelled to the foothills of Iraq to spearhead a series of strategic excavations designed to test the competing hypotheses regarding the origins of domestication. Braidwood's excavations employed a bevy of natural scientists, and the final report questioned the very existence of significant post-Pleistocene climatic shifts in the Near East. Instead, Braidwood and his team found an essentially stable climate during the period of animal and plant domestication, and in light of these data Childe's "oasis theory" was rejected. Braidwood chose to employ a new explanation, which came to be termed the "hilly flanks theory." Rather than looking to environmental causes for the origins of agriculture, Braidwood and his colleagues suggested that a post-Pleistocene readaptation (the Mesolithic) had been unnecessary in the Near East since the climate had not really changed. Instead, agriculture had apparently arisen as a logical outcome of cultural elaboration and specialization. The hunters and gatherers simply "settled in" during the post-Pleistocene, becoming intimately familiar with their plant and animal neighbors. As man's culture evolved further so did more efficient means of exploitation, and agriculture quite naturally formed another link in the long evolutionary chain of mankind. The "hilly flanks theory" is thus an elaboration of the earlier Peake-Fleure model, yet without the climatic elements and environmental deterioration.

Operating from the perspective of theoretical biological ecology, Lewis Binford has recently suggested yet another alternative. In ecological terms, niches must be distinguished from habitats. A *habitat* refers to the organic and inorganic setting in which organisms live, while the way in which they exploit that habitat is termed a *niche*. In simplified terms, an animal's habitat is his address in the environment while his niche is his profession. Binford argues that plant domestication ought to be viewed as merely another of man's ecological niches. In this perspective, man operating within a successful niche would rarely experiment with new and more efficient sources of food. There are many ethnographic cases of hunting-gathering groups such as the California Indians and the groups of the Northeast Atlantic Coast who never grew crops, preferring to live within their traditional foraging subsistence base. Why adapt to some new method when the old one seems to work quite well?

This theory argues that man is motivated to tap a new energy source such as domesticated plants only when he is *forced* to do so. Binford thus rejects Braidwood's notion that agriculture was developed because "culture was ready for it." On this point, Binford is in agreement with Childe in that domestication is a new niche imposed by changing conditions. But while Childe called upon climatic and environmental changes as the initiating factor, Binford proposes that the true stress upon these groups was pressure from other human populations. Specifically, population pressure was exerted by groups of people with extremely successful Mesolithic adaptation who were occupying the same habitat within the Fertile Crescent. The new Mesolithic emphasis upon riverine and lacustrine food sources (fish, shellfish, sea mammals) permitted a sedentary and comparatively lavish existence as opposed to more traditional hunter-gatherer modes of subsistence. The competitive pressures upon the nonsedentary, non-Mesolithic peoples must have been severe, and it is in these marginal areas, Binford suggests, that man was forced to turn to domestication for survival. The Binford theory offers not only a set of plausible conditions, but also relevant motivation for domestication.

Binford's hypothesis not only explains most of the known facts, but it is also directly testable by further archaeological fieldwork. Specifically, Binford's theory predicts (after Wright 1971:461):

1. There must have been a population increase due to a new and efficient Mesolithic lifeway in the optimal zones *prior* to the first domestication.
2. The earliest evidence of domestication should not come from these optimal zones where the Mesolithic lifeway functioned, but rather in the marginal, less favored areas (as the Law of Evolutionary Potential would suggest).
3. The material culture of the earliest Neolithic populations should be essentially similar to their Mesolithic neighbors.
4. There should be no circumscribed *center* of domestication; the process should have occurred simultaneously in several areas under population pressure.

Adequate data for the testing of Binford's ideas are not yet available, but the ecological hypothesis has provided archaeology with an operational set of testable proposals.

The final chapter in the study of early domestication in the Old World has yet to be written, for Binford's recent ideas have not yet received adequate scientific appraisal. Without doubt, Binford's hypothesis will be modified by further work and perhaps even ultimately rejected. At this point, Binford's theory can be compared with MacNeish's initial ideas; neither can be considered validated until confirmed with facts from future excavations. Binford's inductions can only be appraised by how successfully they predict future archaeological finds.

In all, the study of domestication illustrates two points germane to archaeology's quest for cultural processes. The emphasis upon ecological factors is a significant trend in modern archaeology. Binford, and to some extent Childe, consistently views man within the total ecosystem, reacting to external environmental stimuli. Braidwood and others, however, search for causes primarily among internal cultural mechanisms. While neither approach is entirely capable of solving all problems, the changing of focus is significant in modern research. Another notable new direction is toward the explicit use of established scientific methods in the study of cultural processes. MacNeish's success in Mexico and the potential—yet unproven—success of the Binford model in the Near East rest squarely upon the insistence of both archaeologists to follow the steps of the scientific method. Future progress in elucidation of cultural processes may in fact be directly proportional to the reliance upon scientific principles. (For an excellent presentation of the scientific approach to archaeology, see Watson, LeBlanc, and Redman 1971.)

## THE RISE OF CIVILIZATION

Although the domestication of plants and animals was a prodigious step in the evolution of culture, agriculture *per se* is insufficient to fully account for modern culture as we know it. That is, civilization involves more than growing crops and herding animals. Each of us, of course, has an intuitive notion of what "civilized" means, but intuition is inadequate for most scientific purposes. For years paleo-ethnologists have attempted to isolate the fundamental and recurrent elements common to all civilizations. Most of the ancient states, for example, had intensive irrigation complexes capable of supporting massive multicommunity governments. This increased productivity allowed craftsmen the "luxury" of spending all of their time at their craft, rather than having to spend their time procuring food. Trade became an important component of civilized life, and ancient states often developed sophisticated transportation facilities to stimulate the increased regional contact. The very bookkeeping required by trade and taxation acted as a catalyst for the development of writing systems. In fact, the earliest known writing comes from the temples of Uruk where the priesthood evidently administered the huge tithes by means of a series of symbols recorded in clay tablets. The Mesoamerican states evolved ideographic writing and we find their hieroglyphs carved on stelae, altars, and stairways and painted on pottery or in books (codices) made of deerskin or of paper made from the inner bark of trees. Dynastic Egypt evolved a complex calendrical system in order to correlate their critical agricultural practices with the annual flooding of the Nile. Yet even a trait as important as writing cannot be considered universal, for the highly evolved and sophisticated pre-Columbian states of Peru failed to develop writing.[1]

---

[1] One sidelight of some interest is Rafael Larco Hoyle's (1966) claim that the ancient Mochica of Peru actually succeeded in devising a writing system. According to Larco, Mochica runners carried dozens of inscribed beans in small leather pouches. The inscriptions were messages made up of dots, parallel lines, broken lines, and so on. Larco can reportedly find

In fact, there is no single trait which satisfactorily accounts for the development of civilized life, although scholars continue to construct composite lists in the study of cultural evolution (for a review of such attempts, see Steward 1948 and Carneiro, in press).

A recent study by William Sanders and Barbara Price (1968) presents one alternative to the more traditional trait-list approach in the investigations of the dynamics of civilizations. They shift the focus from isolated elements to the *processes* which presumably underly all civilized communities. Sanders and Price view civilization in an explicitly ecological perspective, as merely another of man's cultural adaptations. Each civilization represents an adaptation within its unique ecosystemic matrix. Archaeological and ethnographic data can be more readily compared in this fashion, since the ecological approach is based upon the same premise whether one works with contemporary New Guinea farmers or the remains of a civilization which vanished a thousand years ago. Sanders and Price pose several salient questions in their consideration of the universals of civilized life: "Why were the early civilizations restricted to certain areas?"; "Why were the rates of evolution different in these areas?"; "Can civilization be considered 'inevitable' under given circumstances?" Such heady questions probe at the very heart of modern anthropology and, more germane to this book, they can be answered only through detailed scrutinizing of the archaeological record.

At the outset Sanders and Price (1968:227) summarily state that "civilized society is above all else stratified society." The implication is that at least two subgroups must exist within every civilized society: the rich and the poor. Although archaeologists can never excavate an intact stratified social system, such lifeways leave unmistakable markers for the observant. The construction of monumental architecture, for example, usually implies a viable system of technological controls such as taxation, a corps of specialized craftsmen, and a relatively efficient bureaucracy to administer the entire operation. Thus although the clues come from material culture, the inferences aim specially at processes.

Sanders and Price isolate what they feel to be the three primary processes operative in the evolution of the New World civilization: population growth, competition, and cooperation. Of these *population growth* is considered most fundamental since absolute population size can be interpreted as a measure of society's productive potential. In its most simplified form, this thesis is that "organizational stresses occur as a society increases in size; size is broadly limited by population density, and such stresses stimulate the development of more effective systems of social controls (*i.e., civilizations*)" (1968:84).

With ecological theory close at hand, Sanders and Price then attack the problems of the evolution of civilization in Middle America. Archaeologists working in the rich pre-Columbian ruins of Mexico and Guatemala have traditionally divided the

---

thousands of representations of similarly inscribed beans on pottery and in the famous Nazca and Paracas textiles. Larco felt that Mayan hieroglyphs and the Peruvian ideograms had a common origin. He noted that the Maya word TZIB, meaning "writing," is really comprised of two morphemes: TZ meaning "to draw a line" and IB meaning "a large white bean." It should be noted that most Peruvian scholars question Larco's evidence, and many flatly deny the presence of writing in pre-Columbian Peru.

Mesoamerican culture area into two rather distinct segments. The Mexican Highlands consist of the arid montane basins of central Mexico. The past civilizations of the Teotihuacanos, the Toltecs, and the Aztecs were all born, flourished, and died within the ecological milieu of the Highlands. The second major region lies within the humid jungle habitats of the Yucatan Peninsula and the Gulf Coast Plain, where the Classic Mayan civilization evolved by the second century A.D. and then collapsed some 600 years later.[2]

In its boldest form the Sanders-Price theory attempts to explain how these ecological differences influenced the trajectories of the Mesoamerican civilizations. While the Highland-Lowland dichotomy should not be overdrawn, there seem to be cultural as well as ecological distinctions between the two regions. Probably the most salient difference was *urbanism*. It has been estimated that in its heyday the Highland city of Teotihuacan covered over 19 km. and perhaps hosted a total population of some 85,000 people. A city in the true sense, Teotihuacan contained a "downtown" section complete with market places and a planned urban core which was probably devoted to bureaucratic and sacred functions. A peripheral zone consists of the ruins of several housing complexes, which gradually give way to the outskirts of the city, where the bulk of the Teotihuacanos must have dwelt. Tula, the capital of the later Toltec empire, and the Aztec city of Tenochtitlan (which today lies under the center of modern Mexico City) were also true cities, tightly nucleated and socially stratified. In contrast to this, Sanders and Price feel that the Classic Maya probably lacked urban centers in the strict sense. They suggest that the largest Mayan sites are better characterized as "ceremonial centers," serving both secular and sacred functions but lacking the large stratified populations characteristic of the Highland cities.[3]

Although the farmers of both Highland Mexico and the Lowlands grew primarily corn, beans, and squash, their horticultural technologies were rather different in detail. The Mayans practiced *milpa*, a system of shifting cultivation in which the fields were partially cleared and burnt prior to planting and much of the natural vegetation reduced to ashes. Not only were the fields cleared by burning but the standing biomass was converted to ashes, and the natural nutrients were returned to the soil thereby enriching the productive potential. The swidden method generally requires that the land be left fallow between several years of planting in order to allow the successful growth of the natural vegetation, thus enriching the depleted soil. Depending upon local soil conditions, this fallow interval lasts from a single growing season to decades. According to information from modern *milpa* farmers, 80 to 90 percent of the available land in most areas was out of production in any given year.

[2] Sanders and Price (1968:27) consider the Olmec to be a chiefdom, not a state.

[3] The theory that the Maya lack true cities has been challenged by William Haviland (1970) among others, who argues that Tikal, a massive Mayan site lying some 300 km. north of modern Guatemala City, meets all criteria of urbanism. Haviland estimates that the population may have been as large as 45,000 people. While this is smaller than Teotihuacan and Tenochtitlan in the Highlands, this figure nevertheless compares favorably with the ancient cities of Sumer in the Near East. Haviland also finds enough evidence of economic specialization (farmers, traders, stoneworkers, engineers, astronomers, bureaucrats, etc.) to convince him that Tikal must also have been rather markedly socially stratified.

It should not be concluded, however, that the Maya were cultivators to the exclusion of all other subsistence activities, for there is some evidence that the Maya spared breadnut and zapote trees while clearing the fields, each household maintaining an easy access to these highly nutritious foods (Haviland 1970:194). Wilkin (1971) has studied modern Mayan practices and suggests that the ancients may well have upgraded their agricultural productivity by using the agricultural techniques of terracing and *chinampas* (like the so-called "floating gardens" of modern Xochimilco). It is also quite likely that the Maya collected lakeshore foods and edible plants, exploited marine resources, and often hunted the locally available wild animals, especially deer.

In the Mexican Highlands (especially the basins of Mexico City, Puebla, and upper Balsas) the soil was relatively richer and unencumbered by the dense jungle vegetation typifying the Lowlands. In certain areas of the Highlands the natural processes such as alluviation of montane valleys permitted nearly continuous usage of bottom lands without any form of artificial fertilization. Elsewhere in the Highlands the soil was developed through the addition of animal (and sometimes human) waste products and the organic garbage from nearby farming settlements. But the most significant agricultural advance was the discovery of *floodwater irrigation*, a technique through which suspended particles of soil, organic nutrients, and minerals could be artificially returned to depleted fields. Recent archaeological evidence suggests that irrigation was perhaps practiced in the Teotihuacan Valley by Early Classic times, some 2300 years ago. Sanders and Price feel that the valley slopes may have been terraced and inundated by floodwater in a manner not unlike the Aztec system which Cortes observed in 1519 (1968:149).

The distribution of these two agricultural systems was thus closely correlated with the two primary ecological provinces of Mesoamerica; the Lowland Maya practiced a mixed economy based largely upon *milpa* agriculture while irrigation was restricted to the central valleys of the Highlands. In terms of modern ecological principles, each distinctive habitat apparently required its own equally distinctive niche. But even more important in the study of cultural evolution is that each ecological niche closely conditioned the sociocultural institutions of each group, for the Highlanders lived in cities and yet the Mayans probably did not.

At one time all the Middle American peoples were hunters and gatherers of wild plants who were ignorant of plant domestication. In areas such as the Tehuacan Valley studied by MacNeish, plants were apparently domesticated quite early and as these discoveries passed between groups, the specific agricultural techniques evolved to suit differing habitats. Assuming that early modes of agriculture involved slash-and-burn technology, Sanders and Price (1968:133) suggest that the tropical Lowlands would have been the most favorable environment in Mesoamerica. The more humid areas of the Highlands were intermediate in potential and the arid uplands were probably least favorable due to drought, erosion, and the short growing season. Thus it was the humid jungles which experienced the earliest population growth due to the added productivity of New World agriculture. Yet the available evidence indicates that the earliest experiments in labor-intensive techniques of agriculture took place in ecologically disadvantaged regions of the arid uplands. With the development of more highly productive techniques of floodwater hydroagriculture, the population density of the Highlanders rapidly overtook the Lowland milpa farmers.[4] The cumulative effect of the irrigation process was to nucleate the population, and as the absolute number of people increased so did the population density within the proto-cities.

The rise of urbanism, of course, involved factors other than merely the technology of irrigating one's crops. The groups in areas favorably suited for irrigation quickly gained power and dominated the peoples in areas less well adapted to the new superagriculture. Not only did the irrigationists have a more viable subsistence, but they had the political organization necessary to marshal effective military expeditions for administration of the canals, dikes, and levies. It was necessary to distribute food from the fields to the nonfarming specialists who could be supported in the nonaffluent society. The explosive population growth in time led to extensive trade networks and markets flourished within the inner city. At this point, societies involved in irrigation were firmly stratified into identifiable social classes, which were based largely upon differential access to critical economic resources.

The growth of urban centers has thus tended to accompany hydraulic agriculture, for Highland cities arose only in those areas of Mexico where hydroagriculture was feasible. But the ecology of the Yucatan Lowlands created a rather different situation. The mixed economy based upon *milpa* agriculture supported only a relatively low population density and therefore settlements grew in a rather dispersed fashion. According to Sanders and Price, there was simply not the ecological potential for the progressive cycle of population growth-competition-cooperation witnessed in the Highlands. The largest centers among the Maya were probably ceremonial with only a small resident population comprised primarily of clergy, although Tikal may be an exception. The absence of cities greatly reduced the potential for the social inequity characteristic of more complex societies. Sanders and Price conclude that *left to itself*, the Mayan Lowland region would not have attained civilization. They argue that the Lowland "civilizations without cities" arose as a response to stimuli different from those directing the hydraulic states of the Highlands. At the heart of the Sanders-Price thesis lies the relationship between a strong, aggressive society and its lesser neighbors. The model suggested to explain the nonurban character of Mayan civilization is quite similar to Binford's theory regarding domestication of plants in the Old World. The presence of a powerful society on a small community's borders stimulates the smaller group to readapt itself for survival. In the case of the Maya, this reorganization (evolution, if you will) involved the adoption of the sociopolitical organization of the Highlands. Mayan civilization still required the critical prerequisites for the state (especially a minimal population level and a stable economic base), but the urban sites simply never developed in the Lowlands. The earliest nucleated states of the Mexican Highlands evolved primarily through inner responses to ecological stimuli. The nonurban civilizations also responded to ecological factors, but in this case the form of that response came from outside the existing local fabric of the society. It is clear that Sanders and Price, like Binford, view societies as if they were organisms,

---

[4] Here again is another striking illustration of the Law of Evolutionary Potential, discussed earlier in this chapter.

interacting as part of the ongoing ecosystem, rather than as independent cultural entities operating through vitalistic mechanisms.

## MULTIPLE WORKING HYPOTHESES

This discussion of scientific approaches in anthropology has proceeded largely by example: Richard MacNeish's search for the earliest domestication of Middle American plants, Lewis Binford's study of processes involved in domestication in the Old World, and the William Sanders and Barbara Price discussion of the evolution of civilization in Mesoamerica. In each case the scholar induced a theory which best accounted for the known facts, but only MacNeish's project directly involved the testing of his theory upon new and independent facts. The Sanders-Price and Binford models will rise or fall upon the basis of further archaeological survey, excavation, and analysis of museum collections.

But it is somewhat misleading to consider scientific research as merely the interplay between proposal and testing of isolated hypotheses. The scientific method properly applied should involve the simultaneous framing and testing of many theories. The method of multiple working hypotheses requires the simultaneous testing of several competing theories to continue until all but one is rejected. Binford's hypothesis, you will remember, was proposed as an alternative to both the "oasis theory" of V. Gordon Childe and also Braidwood's "hilly flanks theory." Final scientific judgment will not be bestowed upon the basis of eloquence (or frequency) of presentation, but rather upon the ability of each competing theory to *predict the past*.

Similarly, the Sanders-Price theory is only one of several rival working hypotheses. William Haviland (1970) has analyzed the Mayan site at Tikal and he concludes that urbanism is present without any evidence of irrigation. He feels that Sanders and Price have been misled, for it is not the waterworks *per se* that make irrigation important in the Highlands, but rather the bureaucratic regulation of people that fosters the rise of civilization. By focussing upon the mechanisms of control, irrigation may be considered a sufficient cause of civilization but not a necessary one. Haviland suggests that Mayan religion may have functioned not unlike irrigation in the Highlands to exert the critical control at Tikal. Because of its proficiency with complex calendrical systems, the Mayan priesthood not only held the key to religious phenomena, but they could also predict some of the important seasonal conditions necessary for agriculture. The priests could tell the farmer when to plant his crops and in this manner the ceremonial center controlled to some degree the agricultural hinterland. As the Lowland population increased so did occupational specialization and trading with outside areas, and urban areas like Tikal became necessary to collect and redistribute economic provisions. These alternative modes of social control suggest to Haviland that the hydraulic hypothesis of Sanders, Price, and others is insufficient to explain the rise of Mayan civilization.

Yet a third theory of the origin of civilized society in the New World has been advanced by Robert Carneiro of the American Museum of Natural History. Like Haviland, Carneiro also objects to the hydraulic hypothesis, for there is some evidence of the state actually *preceding* irrigation in Mesoamerica. Additionally, Carneiro terms the hydraulic hypothesis a "voluntaristic" theory, one requiring that "at some point in their history, certain peoples spontaneously, rationally, and voluntarily gave up their individual sovereignties and united with other communities to form a larger political unit deserving to be called a state" (Carneiro 1970:733). While admitting that irrigation probably added to the power of existing states, Carneiro questions whether the mechanisms of irrigation can satisfactorily explain the *origin* of the state. As an alternative working hypothesis, Carneiro proposes his "circumscription theory" which assumes that people only surrender individual autonomy to a state when they are forced to do so, and *warfare* is suggested as the only mechanism powerful enough to forcibly impose bureaucratic authority on a large scale. Yet since warfare does not invariably lead to state formation, Carneiro is quick to add that while necessary, warfare is insufficient in itself to account for the state. It is only in areas where agricultural land is at a premium—areas which are "circumscribed"—that warfare predictably leads to the formation of the state. Only when defeated peoples cannot escape into uninhabited hinterlands and must submit to conquest by their visitors that warfare "causes" the state to evolve.

This sampling of competing theories—and there are several others which could have been discussed—should be sufficient to indicate how science proceeds to identify the truth in anthropology. It should be mentioned in passing, however, that archaeology is a relatively immature science and scholars still become rather firmly (in some cases, inextricably) wed to their "pet theories." Unfortunately, some debates in archaeology are more involved with the intransigent defense of previous ideas rather than the objective appraisal of new data.[5] The method of multiple working hypothesis is a research strategy which urges scientists to simultaneously cultivate as many theories as possible, assiduously withholding personal judgment until all proposals have been adequately tested. Today this method remains an "ideal model" and the practice of archaeology will probably not arrive at cold, detached, and impersonal judgments for some time to come.

## CASE STUDY INTERACTION

I. Binford and MacNeish both studied man's initial efforts to control his environment by domestication of animals and plants. In their boreal forest habitat the Huron grew their own food, primarily maize, while the Washo, living as they did between the lush Lake Tahoe and the high deserts of the Great Basin, were foragers who grew none of their own food. Hunters and gatherers such as the Washo and their Californian neighbors are often well aware of nearby agricultural practices, yet consistently decline to adopt agriculture as their own subsistence base.

    a. From a careful reading of both *The Huron: Farmers of the North* and *Two Worlds of the Washo*, what reasons can you give for the Huron electing to

---

[5] Any reader doubting that scholars become personally and emotionally involved with their theories is urged to consult the autobiographies of some prominent scientists. Especially revealing is *The Double Helix* (1968) by Nobel Prize winner James Watson or *An Archaeological Perspective* (1972) in which Lewis Binford frankly discusses his personal involvement in the evolution of the "new archaeology."

grow crops while the Washo rejected the notion of agriculture? Be certain to consider both the natural and cultural environment of each group.

b. Growing cultigens permitted a rather more stable lifeway than possible under most foraging conditions. What specific advantages did the Huron seem to enjoy over the Washo as a direct result of their agricultural subsistence base? Can you find any disadvantages?

II. The Sanders-Price model linked the development of civilization directly to ecological factors. The Huron, although agricultural, never possessed a civilization as defined by Sanders and Price. Do you feel that if left in isolation, free from disruptive contact with the French and the British, the Huron would have developed a civilization? That is, did the Huron have the *potential* for civilized life, in the strict sense, or were there limiting factors in the Huron lifeway which forever precluded their advancing to civilization?

III. In assessing the scientific method, several rather specific terms were applied to the sequential operations: induction, deduction, and verification. Most frequently in archaeology, however, the investigator never details each step in their testing of anthropological theories, although the steps are implicit in the overall operation. Returning to the discussion of the work of Peter White in New Guinea, analyze the experiment in the following steps of the scientific method:

1. *Induction* of a hypothesis.
2. *Deduction* of specific propositions to be tested.
3. *Verification* and subsequent acceptance or rejection of the initial hypothesis.

# 8

# Horizons of Paleoethnology

We have briefly considered some of the methods through which archaeologists predict the past. We are left with one further prediction—a prophecy for the future of archaeology. Archaeology has undergone rather drastic shifts in orientation over the recent decade, and we are entitled to wonder about the prospects for anthropological archaeology.

In archaeology's recent past, it was possible for an investigator to carry his data in his head. A good archaeologist could often pick up an unidentified artifact and rapidly recite its age, material, geographical distribution, cultural affinities, and context. Such virtuoso performances, while still impressive and often helpful, are becoming less relevant. The modern archaeologist must recognize that the increased complexity of his profession has changed its demands upon the individual scholar. The human mind is no longer the most convenient or reliable means of data storage and recall. Consider, for example, the work performed at the prehistoric Mesoamerican city of Teotihuacan. Literally millions of artifacts were recovered. To analyze the collections the frequency and distribution of artifacts must be analyzed, intricate maps are needed, and artifacts need to be readily classified into both functional and temporal types. So great is the volume of detail involved in this project that without the aid of a computer, the archaeologists would have had to devote several entire lifetimes to the analyses.

The speed and accuracy of modern computers have opened up entirely new areas of research. Projects are now being undertaken which previously would have never been attempted due to the sheer bulk of information involved. Not even the most dedicated archaeologist would (or should) be willing to spend years of his life upon the mindless tedium of manually analyzing the huge samples from projects like that at Teotihuacan, the Reese River, or the New Guinea villages of Hareke and Aluni.

Although computers are attempting humanly impossible simulations of adaptive systems, no machine can replace the archaeologist as field observer or innovative thinker. In the future, the computer doubtless will become a common tool, yet another technique used by the archaeologist in the formulation and investigation of the questions of prehistory.

Probably the most rewarding thrust in current anthropological archaeology is the study of cultural ecology—man's interrelationship with his natural and cultural environments. There have traditionally been two modes of attack upon cultural ecology: by studying man's *perception* of his environment (the "ethnoecological" school) or by focussing upon man's actual, on-the-ground behavior. That is, cultural ecology as a discipline studies both what men *actually* do and also what men *think* they do. Since the archaeologist cannot hope to find fossilized ideas of the past, he is forced to admit at the outset that he can never really view past environments through the eyes of the participant. Archaeologists, in short, cannot elucidate ethnoecology so they must concentrate upon the other kind of cultural ecology; paleoethnologists only consider how people in fact interact with their environment. In the ecological study of the prehistoric Reese River area (Chapter 5), for example, not once were we tempted to refer to what these individuals thought; the prime concern was always with what they actually did. Equipped with this existential outlook, tomorrow's archaeologist is free to explore the relevant problems of paleoecology.

The underlying motivation of all cultural ecologists is to uncover the universals of man-land relationships. In so doing, cultural ecologists are obliged to study the unsuccessful as well as successful adaptations of man. Since unsuccessful adaptations by definition do not survive, few exist in the modern world. Archaeology is the subdiscipline of anthropology best equipped to cope with man's extinct cultural adaptations. *Cultural ecology, therefore, cannot progress without archaeology.* Today, archaeologists are frequently setting aside their shovels and taking their proper place beside the more traditionally recognized ecologists—the zoologists, botanists, entomologists, and others.

Like paleontology and paleobotany, paleoethnology has the unparalleled advantage of studying adaptations over huge spans of time. The perspective of time gives archaeology its greatest tool in the study of *cultural evolution.* We saw how Binford applied an ecological viewpoint in the examination of plant domestication, and how the Sanders-Price model, grounded in a similar ecological perspective, considered the development of civilization in the New World. Such studies project a bright light for the future of archaeology since the evolution of culture can be quite profitably viewed as the succession of more efficient ecological adaptations, the sequential carving of new niches. The extent to which ecological studies can explain the human condition remains to be seen, but at this point archaeology is capable of making valuable contributions to the study of man—who he is today and how he got that way.

## CASE STUDY INTERACTION

I. In emphasizing the strong points of archaeology, we have passed rather quickly over the shortcomings of the archaeological approach. One such limitation mentioned earlier is the impossibility of archaeology recovering the *ideas* of the prehistoric past, since we now realize that both artifact systems and the networks of the mind are much too complex to expect a one-to-one correspondence. As Lewis Binford has emphasized, *paleopsychology* is a task for which modern archaeologists are poorly equipped.

   a. *Two Worlds of the Washo* is an ethnographic monograph based upon months of fieldwork among the modern Washo Indians. In considering the lifeways of prehistoric ancestors of the Washo, the archaeologist of course has no informants; he can only listen to material remains. Archaeological fieldwork can tell much of ecological adaptations, man-land relations, group size, and so forth, but much information is obviously lost. In looking at *Two Worlds of the Washo*, what aspects of Washo life do you feel could *never* be reconstructed without informants? Be certain to discuss both general areas of culture and also rather specific cases.

b.  Repeat this same exercise for *The Huron: Farmers of the North*.

II.  Bruce Trigger emphasized in his Preface that *The Huron: Farmers of the North* is an historical ethnography, relying upon reports of early settlers, missionaries, and government officials rather than upon fieldwork among modern Huron descendents. Historic observers, not trained in anthropological methods, often make the error of projecting their own values upon the customs of others, a shortcoming called *ethnocentrism*. This lack of objectivity often distorted or ignored crucial aspects of aboriginal culture. Trigger mentioned several such omissions and distortions in *The Huron*; discuss these cases, indicating how *archaeological* research could fill in these gaps.

# Bibliography

Beardsley, Richard K., 1956, "Functional and Evolutionary Implications of Community Patterning," *American Antiquity*, 22:129–157.

Binford, Lewis R., 1962, "Archeology as Anthropology," *American Antiquity*, 28:217–225.

———, 1964, "A Consideration of Archeological Research Design," *American Antiquity*, 29:425–441.

———, 1968a, "Archeological Perspectives," in *New Perspectives in Archeology*, Sally R. Binford and Lewis R. Binford, eds., pp. 5–32. Chicago: Aldine Publishing Company.

———, 1968b, "Some Comments on Historical versus Processual Archaeology," *Southwestern Journal of Anthropology*, 24:267–275.

———, 1968c, "Post-Pleistocene Adaptations," in *New Perspectives in Archeology*, Sally R. Binford and Lewis R. Binford, eds., pp. 313–341. Chicago: Aldine Publishing Company.

———, 1972, *An Archaeological Perspective*. New York: Seminar Press.

Carneiro, Robert L., 1970, "A Theory of the Origin of the State," *Science*, 169, 733–738.

———, in press, "The Four Faces of Evolution," in *Handbook of Social and Cultural Anthropology*, John J. Honigmann, ed. Skokie, Ill.: Rand McNally and Company.

Childe, V. Gordon, 1951, *Man Makes Himself*. New York: Mentor Books.

Clarke, David L., 1968, *Analytical Archaeology*. London: Methuen & Co., Ltd.

Cowan, Richard A., 1967, "Lake Margin Ecological Exploitation in the Great Basin as Demonstrated by an Analysis of Coprolites from Lovelock Cave, Nevada," *University of California Archaeological Survey Reports*, No. 70:21–35.

Cowgill, George L., 1970, "Some Sampling and Reliability Problems in Archaeology," in *Archéologie et Calculateurs*, pp. 161–175. Paris: Centre de la Recherche Scientifique.

Crabtree, Don E., 1966, "A Stoneworker's Approach to Analyzing and Replicating the Lindenmeier Folsom," *Tebiwa*, 9:3–39.

———, 1968, "Mesoamerican Polyhedral Cores and Prismatic Blades," *American Antiquity*, 33:446–478.

Deetz, James, 1965, "The Dynamics of Stylistic Change in Arikara Ceramics," *Illinois Studies in Anthropology*, No. 4.

———, 1967, *Invitation to Archaeology*. Garden City, N.Y.: The Natural History Press.

Downs, James F., 1966, *Two Worlds of the Washo*. New York: Holt, Rinehart and Winston, Inc.

Faul, Henry, 1971, "Potassium-Argon Dating," in *Dating Techniques for the Archaeologist*, Henry N. Michael and Elizabeth K. Ralph, eds., pp. 157–163. Cambridge, Mass.: The M.I.T. Press.

Frison, George, 1970, "The Glenrock Buffalo Jump, 48C0304," *Plains Anthropologist*, Memoir 7.

Gentner, W., and H. J. Lippolt, 1969, "The Potassium-Argon Dating of Upper Tertiary and Pleistocene Deposits," in *Science in Archaeology*, 2d ed., Don Brothwell and Eric Higgs, eds., pp. 88–100. New York: Frederick A. Praeger, Inc.

Gould, Richard A., 1966, "Archaeology of the Point St. George Site, and Tolowa Prehistory," *University of California Publications in Anthropology*, Vol. 4.

Gustafson, Carl E., 1968, "Prehistoric Use of Fur Seals: Evidence from the Olympic Coast of Washington," *Science*, 161:49–51.

Haury, Emil W., 1950, *The Stratigraphy and Archaeology of Ventana Cave Arizona*. Tucson: The University of Arizona Press.

Haviland, William A., 1970, "Tikal, Guatemala and Mesoamerican Urbanism," *World Archaeology*, 2:186–198.

Heizer, Robert F., and John A. Graham, 1967, *A Guide to Field Methods in Archaeology: Approaches to the Anthropology of the Dead*. Palo Alto, Calif.: The National Press.

Hill, James N., and Richard H. Hevly, 1968, "Pollen at Broken K Pueblo: Some New Interpretations," *American Antiquity*, 33:200–210.

Hole, Frank, and Robert F. Heizer, 1973, *An Introduction to Prehistoric Archeology*, 3d ed. New York: Holt, Rinehart and Winston, Inc.

Howard, Hildegarde, 1929, "The Avifauna of Emeryville Shellmound," *University of California Publications in Zoology*, 32:378–383.

Jones, Olive, 1971, "Glass Bottle Push-Ups and Pontil Marks," *Historic Archaeology*, 5:62–73.

Kemeny, John G., 1959, *A Philosopher Looks at Science*. New York: Van Nostrand Reinhold Company.

Kleindienst, Maxine R., and Patty Jo Watson, 1956, "Action Archaeology: The Archaeological Inventory of a Living Community," *Anthropology Tomorrow*, 5:35–52.

Larco Hoyle, Rafael, 1966, *Peru*. New York: World Publishing Company.

Lorrain, Dessamae, 1968, "An Archaeologist's Guide to Nineteenth Century American Glass," *Historic Archaeology*, 2:35–44.

MacNeish, Richard S., 1964, "Ancient Mesoamerican Civilization," *Science*, 143:531–537.

Martin, Paul S., 1967, "Prehistoric Overkill," in *Pleistocene Extinctions*, P. S. Martin and H. E. Wright, Jr., eds., pp. 75–120. New Haven, Conn.: Yale University Press.

Michael, Henry N., 1971, "Climates, Tree Rings, and Archaeology," in *Dating Techniques for the Archaeologist*, Henry N. Michael and Elizabeth K. Ralph, eds., pp. 49–56. Cambridge, Mass.: The M.I.T. Press.

Miller, J. A., 1969, "Dating by the Potassium-Argon Method—Some Advances in Technique," in *Science in Archaeology*, 2d ed., Don Brothwell and Eric Higgs, eds., pp. 101–105. New York: Frederick A. Praeger, Inc.

Morris, Ann Axtell, 1933, *Digging in the Southwest*. New York: Doubleday & Company, Inc.

Napton, Lewis K., 1969, "Archaeological and Paleobiological Investigations in Lovelock Cave, Nevada: Further Analysis of Human Coprolites," *The Kroeber Anthropological Society Papers*, Special Publication No. 2.

Peake, Harold, and Herbert John Fleure, 1927, *Peasants and Potters*. London: Oxford University Press.

Ralph, Elizabeth K., 1971, "Carbon-14 Dating," in *Dating Techniques for the Archaeologist*, Henry N. Michael and Elizabeth K. Ralph, eds., pp. 1–48. Cambridge, Mass.: The M.I.T. Press.

Renfrew, Colin, 1971, "Carbon 14 and the Prehistory of Europe," *Scientific American*, 225:63–72.

Rouse, Irving, 1970, "Classification for What?" *Norwegian Archaeological Review*, 3:4–34.

Sahlins, Marshall D., and Elman R. Service, 1960, *Evolution and Culture*. Ann Arbor: University of Michigan Press.

Sanders, William T., and Barbara J. Price, 1968, *Mesoamerica: the Evolution of a Civilization*. New York: Random House, Inc.

Service, Elman R., 1962, *Primitive Social Organization*. New York: Random House, Inc.

Steward, Julian H., 1938, "Basin-Plateau Aboriginal Sociopolitical Groups," *Bureau of American Ethnology Bulletin* 120.

———, 1948, "Cultural Causality and Law: a Trial Formulation of the Development of Early Civilizations," *American Anthropologist*, 51:1–27.

———, 1954, "Types of Types," *American Anthropologist*, 56:54–57.

———, 1970, "The Foundations of Basin-Plateau Shoshonean Society," in *Languages and Cultures of Western North America*, Earl H. Swanson, ed., pp. 113–151. Caldwell, Idaho: Caxton Printers.

Taylor, Walter W., 1948, *A Study of Archeology*. Carbondale: Southern Illinois University Press (reprinted 1967).

Thomas, David Hurst, 1969a, "Great Basin Hunting Patterns: a Quantitative Method for Treating Faunal Remains," *American Antiquity*, 34:392–401.

———, 1969b, "Regional Sampling in Archaeology: a Pilot Great Basin Research Design," *University of California Archaeological Survey Annual Report, 1968–1969*, pp. 87–100. Los Angeles: University of California.

———, 1971a, "On the Use of Cumulative Curves and Numerical Taxonomy," *American Antiquity*, 36:206–209.

———, 1971b, "A Cybernetic Modeling of Historic Shoshoni Economic Patterns," in *Great Basin Anthropological Conference 1970: Selected Papers*, C. Melvin Aikens, ed., pp. 119–134. Eugene: University of Oregon.

———, 1972a, "The Use and Abuse of Numerical Taxonomy in Archaeology," *Archaeology and Physical Anthropology of Oceania*, 7:31–49.

———, 1972b, "A Computer Simulation Model of Great Basin Shoshonean Subsistence and

Settlement Patterns," in *Models in Archaeology*, David L. Clarke, ed., pp. 671–704. London: Methuen & Co., Ltd.

———, 1973, "An Empirical Test of Steward's Model of Great Basin Settlement Patterns," *American Antiquity*, 38:155–176.

Trigger, Bruce G., 1969, *The Huron: Farmers of the North.* New York: Holt, Rinehart and Winston, Inc.

Tugby, Donald J., 1958, "A Typological Analysis of Axes and Choppers from Southeast Australia," *American Antiquity,* 24:24–33.

Watson, James D., 1968, *The Double Helix.* New York: Atheneum Publishers.

Watson, Patty Jo, Steven A. LeBlanc, and Charles Redman, 1971, *Explanation in Archaeology: an Explicitly Scientific Approach.* New York: Columbia University Press.

Weide, Margaret L., 1969, "Seasonality of Pismo Clam Collecting at Ora-82," *University of California Archaeological Survey Annual Report, 1968–1969*, pp. 127–142. Los Angeles: University of California.

White, J. Peter, and David Hurst Thomas, 1972, "Ethno-taxonomic Models and Archaeological Interpretations in the New Guinea Highlands: What Mean These Stones?" in *Models in Archaeology*, David L. Clarke, ed., pp. 275–308. London: Methuen & Co., Ltd.

Wilkin, Gene C., 1971, "Food-Producing Systems Available to the Ancient Maya," *American Antiquity*, 36:432–448.

Willey, Gordon R., and Philip Phillips, 1958, *Method and Theory in American Archaeology.* Chicago: University of Chicago Press.

Willis, E. H., 1969, "Radiocarbon Dating," in *Science in Archaeology*, 2d ed., Don Brothwell and Eric Higgs, eds., pp. 46–57. New York: Frederick A. Praeger, Inc.

Witthoft, John, 1955, "Worn Stone Tools from Southeastern Pennsylvania," *Pennsylvania Archaeologist*, 25:16–31.

Wright, G. A., 1971, "Origins of Food Production in Southwestern Asia: a Survey of Ideas," *Current Anthropology*, 12: 447–477.

# Recommended Reading

This book has taken the position that although archaeologists "do" three different kinds of research—construct cultural chronologies, reconstruct prehistoric lifeways, and study cultural processes—and all three aims are essential to anthropological ends. There is a tremendous bulk of literature dealing with these archaeological procedures, and the following is a highly selective list of sources recommended for the beginning student.

## General Archaeological Theory

Taylor, W. W., 1948, *A Study of Archeology*. Reprinted, Carbondale: University of Southern Illinois Press.

Taylor scolded archaeologists of the pre-World War II era for their obsession with typological trivia and for ignoring the ultimate archaeological goals of archaeology. Taylor's "conjunctive approach" cleared the way for modern paleoanthropology.

Willey, Gordon R., and Philip Phillips, 1958, *Method and Theory in American Archaeology*. Chicago: University of Chicago Press.

American archaeology's most succinct definition of basic concepts. Also contains a brief (and largely out-of-date) summary of New World prehistory.

Rouse, Irving, 1972, *Introduction to Prehistory: A Systematic Approach*. New York: McGraw-Hill Book Company.

A detailed appraisal of modern approaches to archaeological classification, chronology, and culture change.

## Constructing Cultural Chronologies

Michael, Henry N., and Elizabeth K. Ralph (eds.), 1971, *Dating Techniques for the Archaeologist*. Cambridge, Mass.: The M.I.T. Press.

Probably the best handbook on dating techniques currently available to field archaeologists. Discussions of dating by Carbon-14, dendrochronology, archaeomagnetism, thermoluminescence, fission track, potassium-argon, and obsidian hydration.

Hole, Frank, and Robert F. Heizer, 1973, *An Introduction to Prehistoric Archaeology*, 3d ed. New York: Holt, Rinehart and Winston, Inc.

A valuable introduction to technique for the beginner. Ample references so students can find their own answers in the literature.

## Reconstructing Prehistoric Lifeways

Brothwell, Don, and Eric Higgs, 1969, *Science in Archaeology*, 2d ed. New York: Frederick A. Praeger, Inc.

An encyclopedic presentation of how the branches of natural science can help the archaeologist to understand the past. In addition to contributions on dating techniques, this book contains 9 chapters on the analysis of plant remains, 14 chapters on faunal materials, plus comprehensive discussion of soil analysis, microscopy, and statistical methods in archaeology.

Gabel, Creighton, 1967, *Analysis of Prehistoric Economic Patterns*. New York: Holt, Rinehart and Winston, Inc.

A brief consideration of how archaeologists view prehistoric economies. Especially useful for the comprehensive bibliography.

Lee, Richard B., and Irven DeVore, 1968, *Man the Hunter*. Chicago: Aldine Publishing Company.

An intensive survey of the hunting-gathering lifeway. Uses evidence from both archaeological remains and modern ethnographic fieldwork.

*Studying Cultural Processes*

Binford, Sally R., and Lewis R. Binford, 1968, *New Perspectives in Archeology*. Chicago: Aldine Publishing Company.

The first explicit statement by the "new archaeologists." While the papers contribute relatively few substantive insights, their theoretical position has stimulated a generation of archaeologists to operate on paleoanthropology's third (processual) level.

Clarke, David L., 1968, *Analytical Archaeology*. London: Methuen & Co., Inc.

A first-rate presentation of a systems theory approach to archaeology. Clarke's book is difficult reading, indeed, but provides its readers with a sound overview of recent quantitative applications in archaeology.

————, 1972, *Models in Archaeology*. London: Methuen & Co., Ltd.

A varigated compendium of the newest approaches to world-wide archaeological data.

Watson, Patty Jo, Steven A. LeBlanc, and Charles L. Redman, 1971, *Explanation in Archaeology: An Explicitly Scientific Approach*.

The first book directly concerned with relating the philosophy of science to archaeology. It includes considerations of hypothesis-testing, formation of laws, ecological approaches, and a modest introduction to statistical procedures.

# Relevant Case Studies
# in Cultural Anthropology[*]

The annotated lists of sources relevant to this Basic Unit on pages 83 and 84 are furnished as aids to instructors who may want to combine materials from different sources for their courses.

Downs, James F., 1966, *The Two Worlds of the Washo: An Indian Tribe of California and Nevada.* This study reconstructs the traditional tribal culture now lost and analyzes the adaptation to changes wrought by the impact of white culture. It is one of the two Case Studies utilized as basic resources for problems in this Basic Unit.

Downs, James F., 1971, *The Navajo.* This study examines a remote and traditional community (Nez Chi'i) of Navajo where livestock is the basis of life. The material and symbolic aspects of this adjustment are described.

Ekvall, Robert B., 1968, *Fields on the Hoof: Nexus of Tibetan Nomadic Pastoralism.* The *aBrog Pa*, an "altitude zone" pastoral society in Tibet, is described. The various streams of cultural development comprising present-day culture are discussed, including those developed in sedentary communities, high-altitude environment adaptations, and earlier hunting adaptations. The emphasis is on the way in which the people manage to live, with their livestock, at this high altitude.

Hudson, Alfred B., 1972, *Padju Epat: The Ma'anyan of Indonesian Borneo.* This is one of the most complete descriptions of swidden horticultural technology in the Case Study series and deals also with the wider social, economic, and ecological dimensions of this very important form of subsistence.

Rivière, Peter G., 1971, *The Forgotten Frontier: The Cattlemen of Roraima.* This study describes an isolated Brazilian ranching community close to the Venezuelan border. The author analyzes the economic, environmental, ecological, and historical factors that have affected cattle raising and ranching in an area very similar to the bygone "Wild West" of North America.

Spindler, George D., 1973, *Burgbach: Urbanization and Identity in a German Village.* This study focuses on the persistence of traditional forms of adaptation to the land and of particular forms of cultivation in a recently peasant society, now urbanizing rapidly.

[*] Edited by George and Louise Spindler, and published by Holt, Rinehart and Winston, Inc.

# Other Relevant Books[*]

Gabel, Creighton, 1967, *Analysis of Prehistoric Economic Patterns.* Though taking a different approach than does David Hurst Thomas in this Basic Unit, this study from the Studies in Anthropological Method series shows how archaeological data used to draw inferences about population size and density, land use, crafts and labor, trade, and technology. Useful for a comparison of approaches to common problems in archaeology and their results.

Hickerson, Harold, 1970, *The Chippewa and Their Neighbors: A Study in Ethnohistory.* Though primarily concerned with the ways in which ethnohistory sheds light on the past, there is much in this Anthropological Method study that is relevant to this Basic Unit, including discussions of biological-ecological conditions that affected the development of Chippewa communities and their interaction with others in the area.

Oswalt, Wendell H., 1972, *Habitat and Technology.* The author undertakes a systematic analysis of the artifacts of technologically primitive peoples and develops a novel taxonomy that permits precise comparison. Tools, shelter, implements, clothing, and cultivated foodstuffs are included. This is a unique approach, and again furnishes good comparative perspective on the approach developed in this Basic Unit.

Trigger, Bruce G., 1968, *Beyond History: The Methods of Prehistory.* This study stresses the methods used in reconstructing the history of societies that lack written records. Applications are made to Egyptian prehistory. Useful also for comparison of different approaches to common problems.

The Editors

[*] Published by Holt, Rinehart and Winston, Inc.